Managing a Vision
Democracy, Development and Governance

Rs. 750

ISBN: 81-7835-354-7

Published in 2005 in India by
Kalpaz Publications,
C-30, Satyawati Nagar, Delhi-110052
E-mail : Kalpaz@hotmail.com

Laser Typesetting at : Shiva Infosystem, Delhi
Printed at : Mehra Offset Press, Delhi

DEDICATION

A centenary tribute
to a *YUGA PURUSH*

Thinker, Visionary, Social Engineer

Revolutionary who stood firmly against
British imperialism, Muslim separatism
Hindu communalism and Extremism in all its
manifestations

Defender of Democracy

Pioneer of Peace Movement
Patriot without a Parallel

Who gave all, ... his life,
In the service of the nation

a *Karmayogi* of resurgent India
who prompted the Father of the Nation
Mahatma Gandhi to say
'JP married socialism not Prabhavati"

Lok Nayak JAYA PRAKASH NARAYAN
[11 Oct. 1902 – 8 Oct. 1979]
and his consort
'PRABHAVATI *JI*'

In grateful remembrance of the privilege of association when 'JP' had commissioned a study on Communal Conflict (1964-65) and when 'JP' was Chairman of the National Integration Committee (1965-67).

FOREWORD

Dr. G.R.S. Rao is a lucent jurist, and his book a profound classic. Every page has a message, and as we read each chapter, we behold the author's vision of the Indian Constitution, his conception of the mission of the Founding Fathers, and his critical perception of the progression and regression, democracy and development, distortion of the power process and the quantum of participation of the people in the governance of the nation. What a serendipitous work is 'Managing a Vision' where Dr. G.R.S. Rao unfolds with passion and erudition the zig-zag march of our Constitutional Democracy during the last five decades. I am privileged to pen a brief Foreword to his original assessment of the Constitution-in-action, the performance of the players, and the Tryst with Destiny India made as it awoke to Freedom at the stroke of the midnight hour in the middle of August 1947.

The spread of the book is vistaramic and is unique in its creative contribution to a deeper understanding of our National Character. Dr. Rao does not attempt a textbook dealing with the articles of the Constitution, nor does he launch on long essays with judgements of the Supreme Court as jurisprudential meat. On the contrary, he transports us to lofty heights adopting a civilizational perspective, and value-based objective taking us through an integral yoga of history and futurity. He quotes Sardar Patel to prove this point about Freedom as an event and its perils as a portent.

"A great change has come about, a great revolution has been brought into being. This is the first time in history, after centuries, that India can call itself an integrated whole in the real sense of term. But we must all resolve that whatever mistakes we might commit, we should do nothing which would be calculated to send India back into the slavery of the past. It is therefore, the duty of India's valiant sons to see that the clocks of progress are not put back but advance forward". (P-1/2)

Indeed, Dr. Rao beautifully condenses the pith and substance of the book in a couple of paragraphs, which I borrow for easy reference :

"The polyglot society that is India, characterized by continental size, racial milieu, ethnic variety, cultural diversity, linguistic multiplicity, religious pluralism, rural-urban hiatus not to speak of wide variations in the socio-cultural status of people based on age and sex, and historical factors such as feudalism, mutations of caste, and economic disparities offers a complex and fascinating situation for any observer to look at from a wide variety of angles. The people of this polyglot society secured political freedom, and gave unto themselves a Constitution providing not merely the instrumentalities of governance, but also the goals of political, economic, social and cultural freedom as the agenda for social transformation.

The vision of a democratic pluralist polity was aimed at integrating people, paupers and princes alike, as citizens of the Republic, harmonizing fragmented identities, conflicting interests and fractured values. The Constitution of India mapped out the meaning of political freedom. It has envisioned bringing about revolutionary transformation in an evolutionary mode with clearly demarcated milestones, while maintaining a dynamic equilibrium through an inherently Indian ethos of consensual process". (P-2)

It is not my purpose to summarise in abbreviation the large volume of material assembled and arranged methodically. I mean to appetite the reader into the wealth of thought, the functional critique of the Constitutional Process, with its ideological content, the deficits in performance, the 'economic heights and social sights, the deficiencies in peoples participation and the dynamic democracy which is the desideratum of the constitutional order.

We get in Dr. Rao's early pages some idea of the stupendous task which faced the Consembly, the statesmanship of the architects, and the successful consensus arrived at by the House. Poverty and privation, which the vast masses were afflicted with, would have made socialism imperative but the rigidity of ideology was avoided. Ananthasayanam Ayyangar explained :

> "in regard to the economic field, I would have very much liked an enunciation that we are trying to usher in a Democratic Socialistic Republic. But later on, by various clauses in the Directive Principles we have remedied the rigours of capitalism, there is ample provision in this Constitution, which if worked well, will ere long usher in a socialistic democratic republic in this country". (P-8)

I must express my anguish at the Consembly's ambiguity and obviation of democratic socialism, making Directive Principles of State Policy crimson and fundamental in governance, yet non-justiceable. Toothlessly socialistic! The 42nd Amendment declared, in formal terms, our Republic was Secular and Socialist. On federalism Dr. Ambedkar asserted the need for federal structure; nevertheless, he defended a dominant Centre, especially during Emergency. Weak and meek States, and a resource-rich and legislatively strong Union may be simulacrum of federalism. The Judiciary too has an omnipotent Delhi heavy weight. Democracy, in so vast and variegated a country, needs more decentralisation and institutions responsive and sensitive to humble people's aspirations.

The chapter on Constitutional Deficit is luminous and correctionally instructive. A holistic approach to the constitutional deficit in India has been discussed at learned length with special reference to distortions of vision, faulted processes of power, and the backlash of sick governance on the spirit of constitutionalism. Every constitutional jurist and political scientist in India will do well to organise a debate on the various dimensions and deficiencies highlighted in this chapter.

The book concludes with Dr. Rao's thought on Tryst with Destiny. There is a lovely analysis of the evolutionary character of the constitutional order. Dr. Rao has correctly spelt out the institutional identities and their interaction. His words deserve a quote :

> "The Preambular statement sets out the primordial values that constitute the polestar constantly guiding our Republican journey. The Directive Principles similarly inspire the direction and quality of social transformation. They are designed to inspire and shape the process of public policy. There cannot be any doubt that merely because they are not enforceable they can be trampled upon. Just as Mahatma Gandhi had stated, "when in doubt, hold a talisman"; similarly, whenever there is any doubt about the Articles of the Constitution, the legislators have to reflect upon the spirit of the Constitution embedded in the Preamble and the Directive Principles. While the Supreme Court has been assigned the role of arbiter and interpreter, with advisory Jurisdiction on the letter of the Constitution, the President is assigned the sacred and ultimate task of preserving, protecting and defending the

letter, and spirit of the Constitution. The powers and authority vested in the Supreme Court thus do not impinge upon the "role assigned to the President as the protector and defender of the Constitution". (P107)

The final vision of the author is his firm Jeffersonian conviction that the safest depository of the ultimate powers of the State are the people themselves. Even if something goes wrong the remedy is not to withdraw the power from the people-that is despotism-but to inform their consciousness with more enlightenment. Then does the finest hour of democracy arrive and operate.

Cochin **V.R. KRISHNA IYER**

May 24, 2004

PREFACE

We have made significant strides during the first five decades of constitutional democracy though far short of our national endowment. There were democratic countries for centuries but most of them operated as democracies at home and empires outside. Some others were content with winning freedom for themselves. It was India that triggered the movement for political freedom and democracy on a global scale during the 20th century.

The vision of democratic India was inspired by the universal values of liberal democratic governance and human development. These values have to be translated into a reality over decades, and enriched across centuries and cultures. Decades provide milestones for mid-course appraisal and correction. The set of issues reflected upon in this canvas revolve round the management of institutions of governance and process of development. The cardinal issues are : (1) validation and renewal, or mid-course correction of the vision in an evolutionary mode (2) mission mode of managing the institutions, including performance of the players and the umpires; nature of complementarity and interface management; (3) nature and degree of fulfilment of social transformation – progression or regression, and (4) a critical look at the nature of constitutional deficit, warranting fresh managerial inputs as a prerequisite for the 'tryst with destiny'.

As I had tried to grapple with the innumerable issues emerging from the debate on managing India's vision, and the mission mode of governance I thought I must steer clear of the temptation of making fragmented micro-judgements *a la* the eight blind men describing an elephant. The other extreme would be an attempt to capture the elephant into a macro-frame of generalities. As a citizen, I was confident of one advantage : that my fellow citizens of India to whom this is addressed are equipped to fit my random reflections into the multi-dimensional canvas that the Constitution of India presents. I have adopted an illustrative rather than empirical and conceptual approach.

My qualification to make a social audit statement on the Constitution emerges from the fact that I had never worked as a functionary, within any of the institutions of state. As a citizen, and as a professional consultant operating from outside the system, my observations, hopefully provide a mirror view for those who operated the system as legislative, executive, judicial and other functionaries. My first impression is that these functionaries together edged out the people of India from a creative role in the management of the national vision. The citizens of India were deprived thus far, even the feeling that they have a participatory role in the processes of democracy, development and governance.

Democracy is a dynamic process. *Demos,* the people, provide and maintain the gravity to this dynamic process through participation. This brief social audit statement is intended to aid the citizens of India participate in such a creative interaction and thus help maintain the gravity of Indian society as a dynamic constitutional democracy, engaged in the mission of managing the national vision.

Hyderabad **G.R.S. Rao**

August 15, 2004

ACKNOWLEDGEMENTS

Shri. S.V. Raju, President, Indian Liberal Group, Prof. I. V. Chalapati Rao and Prof. B. Ramesh Babu offered their critic and suggestions on the first draft. Dr. B.G. Siddharth, Director General of the Birla Science Museum helped in an appreciation and adaptation of some of the technological terminology.

Ms. N. Suseela and Shri. Mohan of Shasi Services and Shri P. Lakshmi Narayana helped in preparation and several revisions of the manuscript. Shri. L. Prakash of Prakash Digital Studio helped in the graphic presentation of illustrations. Sumita Rao inspired the cover design.

Shri Amit Garg, Director Publications of the Gyan Books undertook the publication and executed the job elegantly as well as expeditiously.

I am beholden to the eminent Jurist Justice Shri V.R. Krishna Iyer, who blessed me with the Foreword.

A project of this nature could not have been conceived and executed without due encouragement from professional colleagues and well wishers. The credit for having been able to complete the project goes to all of them, yet the shortcomings, of which there are many, are entirely to be laid at my doors.

Hyderabad **G.R.S. Rao**

May 16, 2004

1

MOVEMENT FOR FREEDOM

Universal and Eternal Values

What is the meaning and relevance of the 'freedom movement' and 'political freedom' in the context of India which represents a civilisational continuum? One of the most ancient of extant civilisations on this planet with *Sanatana Dharma* as the dominant culture and way of life from times immemorial, exposed to the exploits by waves of political-economic, religious and military campaigns from across its boundaries, this land of ancients demonstrated and stands as a living example of constant absorption and synthesis. India stands out, perhaps, as the only stream of civilisation, that while absorbing and synthesising, it has demonstrated during the 20th Century, its catholicity by peacefully exterminating external domination and asserting its urge for renewal for itself triggering the subjugated communities around the globe to move on the path of freedom, on a universal basis. Twentieth century marked the renaissance of India, the resurgence of an ancient civilisation into a modern nation, with pluralism as the sheet anchor, and socio-economic and cultural freedom as the agenda for *Sampoorna Swaraj*, freedom in its holistic sense.

Sardar Vallabhbhai Patel put the challenge and opportunity before our country in a historical perspective : "if you look at the history of India, you will find that for centuries India was steeped in slavery. What struggles, what sacrifices, what bitterness and what sorrow we all had to face to rid India of that centuries-old malady that had eaten into the very vitals of its nationhood! A great change has come about, a great revolution has been brought into being. This is the first time in history, after centuries, that India can call itself an integrated whole in the real sense of the term. But we must all resolve that whatever mistakes we might commit, we should do nothing which would be calculated to send India back into the slavery of the past. It is therefore, the duty of India's valiant sons to see that the clock of progress is not put back but advances forward".[1] Establishing territorial integration and integrity represented the realisation of a dream, and the dawn of India's freedom.

The polyglot society that is India, characterised by continental size, racial milieu, ethnic variety, cultural diversity, linguistic multiplicity, religious pluralism, rural-urban hiatus not to speak of wide variations in the socio-cultural status of people based on age and sex, and historical factors such as feudalism, mutation and multiplication of caste, and economic disparities offers a complex and fascinating situation for any observer, to look at from a wide variety of angles. The people of this polyglot society secured political freedom, and gave unto themselves a Constitution providing not merely the instrumentalities of governance but also set out the vision of political, economic, social and cultural freedom as the agenda for social transformation.

The substance of the vision of India operates as a touchstone of liberal democracy, movement towards '*Sampoorna Swaraj*', and '*Abhyudaya*', progression of freedom. It was with this agenda that the people of India constituted themselves into a Sovereign

Democratic Republic in 1950, with a blue-print for social transformation; economic freedom [freedom from hunger, malnutrition, deprivation, inhuman levels of poverty, myriad forms of exploitation] and social development [freedom from discrimination, religious bigotry, untouchability and the like]. India's Constitution sets out the route-map for humanist progress. Indeed, India's vision of freedom ignited ripples, and waves of freedom and democracy on a global scale; it set out global standards of freedom and democracy.

The vision of a democratic pluralist polity was aimed at integrating people, paupers and princes alike, as citizens of the Republic, harmonising fragmented identities, conflicting interests and fractured values. The Constitution of India mapped out the meaning of political freedom. It has envisioned bringing about revolutionary transformation in an evolutionary mode with clearly demarcated milestones, while maintaining a dynamic equilibrium through an inherently Indian ethos of consensual process. India's political freedom was not an end in itself, it marked the beginning of an arduous journey on the path of constitutional democracy and humanist progress.

India's civilisational and universalist perspective of freedom was sharply brought out by Sisir Kumar Mitra : "Today India stands on the threshold of a new era, when her spirit, revived by a century of effort, and strengthened by the assimilation of new ideas and ideals, faces the world. The great question for the future is : can India by her conscious effort carry forward to greater summits of achievement the spirit she has inherited through the five thousand years of unbroken succession?" [2]

References

1. Sardar Vallabhbhai Patel, The Constitution and the Constituent Assembly : Lok Sabha Secretariat, New Delhi 1990, p. 96.
2. Sisir Kumar Mitra, Evolution of India : Its Meaning, Jaico Publishing, Bombay, 1968.

2
VISION OF INDIA

Who are the people who envisioned the future of India, and what are the cardinal features and elements of the 'vision'? What is the process adopted in carving out the vision, and the process conceived by them to translate the vision into a reality? The Constituent Assembly provided, and proved to be, the point of convergence that culminated in a synergic mode of sculpting the vision of India. Constitution of India captured the canvas, carved out the vision of India, and set out the modalities.

2.1. The Visionaries

The Constitution is the product of 348 people working together in the Constituent Assembly (Consembly in short). It is a document inspired by 300 millions of Indians who waged a united, non-violent movement in pursuit of political freedom, democratic governance and social change. The substance of such social transformation emerged and the process of change initiated during the freedom movement itself. Thus it would be erroneous to imagine that the Constitution reflected the vision of the 348 members of the Consembly; they had articulated the vision of the freedom movement. The distinctive characteristic of the Consembly and of the founding fathers lies in the fact that they captured the minds and hearts of the 300 millions of people, their aspirations and dreams. At the outset the members of the Consembly solemnly pledged that "unless and until each and every Indian breathes the air of freedom and his miseries are banished and his hard lot is improved our task remains unfinished".[1]

Reflecting on the vitality and longevity of any constitution, and the task before the Consembly, Dr. Sachidananda Sinha the provisional Chairman drew the attention of the members to the celebrated book, titled "Commentaries on the Constitutions of United States" and the striking and inspiring observations of its author who was an eminent Jurist Joseph Story: "Let the American youth never forget, that they possess (in their constitution) a noble inheritance, brought by the toils and sufferings, and blood of their ancestors; and capable, if wisely improved and faithfully guarded, of transmitting to their latest posterity all the substantial blessings of life, the peaceful enjoyment of liberty, property, religion and independence. The structure has been erected by architects of consummate skill and fidelity; its foundations are solid; its compartments are beautiful, as well as useful; its arrangement are full of wisdom and immortality, if the work of man may justly aspire to such title. It may, nevertheless, perish in an hour by the folly or corruption or negligence of its only keepers, THE PEOPLE. Republics are created – by the virtue, public spirit and intelligence of the citizens. They fall, when the wise are banished from the public councils because they dare to be honest and the profligate are rewarded because they flatter the people, inorder to betray them".[2] Upon his election as Chairman of the Consembly, Dr. Rajendra Prasad expressed his sanguine hope that the Members will place before the world "a model of a constitution that will satisfy all our people, all groups, all communities, all religions inhabiting this vast land,

and which will ensure to everyone freedom of action, freedom of thought, freedom of belief and freedom of worship, which will guarantee to everyone freedom in all respects. Above all, what we need is freedom and as some one has said "Nothing is more valuable than the freedom to be free". Let us hope and pray that as a result of the labours of this Constituent Assembly we shall have achieved that freedom and we shall be proud of it".[3]

"A brief survey of the draft constitution must convince the members that it is based upon sound principles of democratic government and contains within itself elements necessary for growth and expansion and is in line with the most advanced democratic constitutions of the world. It is well to remember that a constitution is after all what we make of it"[4] reflected Alladi, on the salient features of the Constitution. "Our constitution is not a mere declaratory document it sets out a process of shaping human values, relations and material conditions of life",[5] observed O.V. Alagesan another member of the Consembly. The vision of the Constitution of India represented a revival and renewal on one hand and enrichment on the other, in order to make it not merely contemporary, but adequate and appropriate for the progress of human condition in India. Though ideologically there were three streams of thought and options viz., Gandhian *Swadeshi*, Nehruvian socialism and Rajaji's free enterprise, the vision of India was not dogmatised. The founding fathers had consciously avoided use of expressions such as 'socialism' and 'secularism'.

Adverting to the Objectives Resolution, Dr. Radhakrishnan visualised the social transformation apart from remaking the material conditions, "we have to safeguard the liberty of the human spirit. It is no good creating conditions of freedom without producing a sense to grow to its fullest stature. The progress of man is due to the play of his mind, now creating, now destroying, always transmuting. We must safeguard the liberty of the human spirit against the encroachments of the state. While state regulation is necessary to improve economic conditions, it should not be done at the expense of the human spirit".[6] Reflecting their faith in the people of India, Alladi Krishnaswami Ayyar observed : "in spite of the ignorance and illiteracy of the large mass of the Indian people, the Assembly has adopted the principle of adult franchise with an abundant faith in the common man and the ultimate success of democratic government on the basis that adult suffrage will bring enlightenment and promote the well-being, the standard of life, the decent living of the common man".[7]

The process of carving out a unified vision was facilitated by a multitude of factors. The 348 members of the Consembly representing the people of India participated in the common cause of freedom movement, the spirit of the movement fusing their thoughts, focussing them towards the citizens of India. The members of the Consembly were creative leaders, transcedental in their disposition, and internalised the Indian ethos of consensualism. The Constituent Assembly may have seen the intellectual titans clash, but their thought process jelled them into a 'team India'.

India's constitution is quintessentially democratic in character : As Ananthasayanam Ayyangar had observed, "it vests the sovereignty in the people and enables them to continue to exercise that sovereignty in full".[8] Responding to the criticism and reservation expressed by some Members about universal adult suffrage, Alladi Krishnaswami Ayyar observed that "More than any other provision in the Constitution, I should think the boldest step taken by this Assembly is in the matter of universal adult suffrage with a belief in the common man and in his power to shape the future of the country".[9] Endorsing the British Prime Minister Attlee's observation, that "in the mass of Asia, an Asia ravaged by war, we have here the one country that has been seeking to apply the principles of democracy. I have always felt myself that political India might be the light of Asia", Dr. S. Radhakrishna adds : "nay the light of the world giving to its distracted mind an integral vision and to its bewildered will an upward direction".[10]

The founders had demonstrated their wisdom and foresight by recognising the futuristic potential of science and technology, the demands of equity between generations, and a dynamic equilibrium of change. Science and technology have been seen as the triggers of rapid social transformation. They had envisaged that the change triggered by the Constitution itself warrants review and reform of the Constitution as a parallel process in an evolutionary mode. Thus they provided appropriate provisions within the Constitution, for reform. Repudiating the charge that the Constitution is rigid, Dr. Ambedkar observed : "one has only to study the provisions for amendment contained in the American and Australian Constitutions. Compared to them those contained in the draft Constitution will be found to be the simplest. The draft Constitution has eliminated the elaborate and difficult procedures such as a decision by a convention or a referendum. The powers of amendment are left with the legislatures, central and provincial. It is only for amendments of specific matter – and they are only few that the ratification of the state legislatures is required. All other Articles of the Constitution are left to be amended by the Parliament. The only limitation is that it shall be done by a majority of not less than two-thirds of the members of each House present and voting and a majority of the total membership of each house. It is difficult to conceive a simpler method of amending the Constitution". Elaborating on the issue, Dr. Ambedkar argued : "what is said to be the absurdity of the amending provisions is founded upon a misconception of the position of the Consembly and of the future Parliament elected under the Constitution. The Consembly had no partisan motive in making a Constitution. Apart from the desire for securing a good and workable Constitution it has no axe to grind. In considering the Articles of the Constitution it has no eye on getting through a particular measure. Members of the future Parliament, if it met as a Constituent Assembly, will be acting as partisans seeking to carry amendments to the Constitution to facilitate the passing of party measures which they have failed to get through by reason of some Article of the Constitution. Parliament will have an axe to grind while the Consembly has none. That is the difference between the Constituent Assembly and the future Parliament. That explains why the Consembly though elected on limited franchise can be trusted to pass the Constitution by simple majority, and why the parliament though elected on adult suffrage cannot be trusted with the same power to amend it".[11]

In constituting any assembly to decide a new constitutional structure the first problem is to obtain as broad based and accurate a representation of the whole population as is possible. The British Cabinet Mission Plan (16 May 1946) proposed that "there shall be elected by each provincial legislative assembly, representatives, each part of the legislative assembly (General, Muslim, Sikh) electing its own representatives by the method of proportional representation with a single transferable vote". But the Consembly so constituted transcended the ethos of proportional representation and created a landmark by adopting a consensual process in framing the Constitution.

The most important task before the Consembly was to secure the political consolidation of the nation. The Cabinet Mission and the Viceroy proposed that an advisory committee be set up by the Constituent Assembly to deal with the rights of citizens, minorities and tribal and excluded areas. Sardar Vallabhbhai Patel was appointed Chairman of this advisory committee. The committee was faced with the question of reservation of seats for the minorities in the legislatures, central and provincial. The committee decided against providing for any reservation for the Muslim minority community. The report of the committee was presented to the Consembly in May 1949. Speaking on the occasion Jawaharlal Nehru spoke thus : "I wish to associate myself with this historic turn in our destiny . . . It means not only discarding something that was evil, but turning upon it and determining with all our strength that we shall pursue a path which we consider fundamentally good for every part of the nation. There is some point in having a safeguard where there is autocratic or foreign rule. As soon as you get something that can be called political democracy, then reservation, instead of helping the party to be safeguarded or aided, is likely actually to turn against it and isolate if from the main current . . . at the cost of forfeiting that inner sympathy and fellow feeling with majority . . . it is not good from the point of view of the majority either. The only way to proceed about it, from the point of view of the minority or the majority, is to remove every barrier, which separates them in the political domain so that they develop and work together. I think that doing away with this reservation business is not only a good thing in itself, good for all concerned, more especially for the minorities, but psychologically too it is a very good move for the nation and the world. It shows that we are really sincere about this business of having a secular democracy. We have each one of us to try to function in a way so as to gain the goodwill of the other group or individual. This is an act of faith for all of us, an act of faith above all for the majority community because they have to show after this that they can behave towards others in a generous, fair and just way. Let us live up to that faith".[12] As Granville Austin observed, "Through her age-old ability to synthesise cultures, assembly members believed, India could become modern, yet remain Indian".[13]

2.2. The Vision

We the people of India constituted ourselves into a Sovereign Democratic Republic, with the Constitution as a blue-print for social transformation. The Indian Constitution has captured the canvas of liberal democracy, providing an integral frame for the vision of India. The vision is neither an utopia, nor a 'wish list' but represented the finer values of humanist progress, a response to the hopes and aspirations of a multitude of humanity. Moving the objectives resolution in the Consembly Nehru observed that it constitutes the high adventure of giving shape, in the printed and written word, to a nation's dream and aspirations. He opined that "it is a Resolution, and yet, it is much more than a resolution. It is a Declaration. It is a firm resolve. It is a pledge and an undertaking and it is for all of us I hope is a dedication" and that, "I can't say that this Resolution at all conveys the passion that lies in the hearts and the minds of the Indian people today".[14] The cardinal propositions of the Resolution are :

1. Establishment of an Independent Sovereign Republic and to draw up Constitution for her future governance.

2. Independent Sovereign India shall be a union.
3. Autonomy of units, together with residuary powers, save and except such powers and functions as are vested in the union.
4. Recognition of the people of India as the sovereign source of all powers.
5. Ensuring Justice, social, economic and political, equality and freedom for the citizens of India.
6. Adequate safeguards for the tribal and backward communities and minorities.
7. Integrity of the territory and sovereign rights.
8. Contribution to the promotion of world peace and welfare of mankind.

Projecting the objectives resolution as the vision of the Constitution, Alladi Krishnaswami Ayyar observed : "the expression 'justice, social, economic and political' while not committing this country and the assembly to any particular form of polity coming under any specific designation, is intended to emphasise the fundamental aim of every democratic state" in the contemporary times, containing "the necessary elements of growth and adjustment needed for a progressive society".[15] Syed Muhammad Saadulla referred to the eight Articles of the Objectives Resolution as "the yardstick to measure the contents of the draft constitution[16] "The Consembly had a clear vision, encompassing a set of values and ideals that would constitute the pole-star for the Republic". Our ideal is to have a constitution that will enable the people's will to be expressed and enforced, and that will not only secure liberty to the individual but also reconcile and make that liberty subservient to the common good",[17] observed Dr. Rajendra Prasad. The Consembly recognised that an ideology is transient and is subject to the process of reciprocity of factors in the process of social change. This was clearly reflected in the observations of Ananthasayanam Ayyangar when he commented : "in regard to the economic field, I would have very much liked an enunciation that we are trying to usher in a Democratic Socialistic Republic. But later on, by various clauses in the Directive Principles we have remedied the rigours of capitalism, there is ample provision in this Constitution which if worked well will ere long usher in a socialist democratic republic in this country".[18] Rebutting the criticism that the common man is ignored and that there is no socialistic flavour about the Constitution, Alladi Krishnaswami Ayyar argued that "while it does not commit the country to any particular form of economic structure or social adjustment, gives ample scope for future legislatures and the future parliament to evolve any economic order and to undertake any legislation they choose in public interest".[19]

The Preamble to the Constitution crystalised the general purpose for which the people ordained and established the Constitution.

"We the people of India, having solemnly resolved to constitute India into a Sovereign Democratic Republic and to secure to all its citizens;

Justice, social, economic and political;

Liberty of thought, expression, belief, faith and worship;

Equality of status and of opportunity and to promote among them all;

Fraternity assuring the dignity of the individual and the unity and integrity of the nation".

The Preamble has been hailed as the soul of the Indian Constitution prescribing human rights and dignity of citizens on a continuing basis. It optimises the highest values of humanity. Apart from the preambular statement, the Directive Principles of State Policy (Annexure-I) vividly set out the aims and objects operating as a pole-star and a touchstone of social transformation. There was some criticism on the ground that the Directive Principles are only pious declarations and that they have no binding force. But Dr. Ambedkar, reflecting on the salient features of the Constitution, maintained thus : "I am not prepared to concede that they are useless because they have no binding force in law".[20] Elaborating his argument Dr. Ambedkar commented thus: "whoever captures power will not be free to do what he likes with it. In the exercise of it, he will have to respect these Directive Principles. He cannot ignore them. He may not have to answer for their breach in a court of law. But he will certainly have to answer for them before the electorate at election time".[21] The Constitution provided a blue-print for social transformation and promised the fruits of political freedom; "that will bring food to our starving people, clothing for them, housing for them and all manner of opportunities of progress, that it will lead also to the freedom of the other countries of Asia",[22] ushering India as a model for democracy.

The Directive Principles are formulated on the recognition that it was not possible to confer economic rights immediately on millions of people over-night. Yet, the Directive Principles reflect the will and aspirations of the people on the basic socio-economic goals of the country. Thus, though they are not enforceable, public policy can't go against them either. As S M Mehta observed, the Directive Principles were intended as "moral precepts for the authorities of the state – they have atleast an educative value". [23]

While carving out the Vision of India, the Constituent Assembly had recognised that social change/development/reform is dynamic, evolutionary and progressive, integrative and universal especially in relation to the populations aspiring to move in the direction of liberal democracy.

Social transformation involves disturbance of the status quo, unsettles a steady state moving towards a state of dynamic equilibrium, transforms not only the structure of the economy but also the social order, creates new opportunities and unleashes unforeseen and unintended problems and challenges. Social transformation is progressive and thus evolutionary on the one hand, and yet integrative and concurrent on the other. Political freedom, liberal democratic order, economic growth and human development cannot be pursued all at once, nor pursued in isolation or in a sequential order. They are interactive and interdependent hence concurrent. Social transformation has also to be integrative – the macro and the micro, as much as the rural and the urban. In the ultimate analysis, it has to meet all these parameters inorder to be sustainable. The vision of India captures all these facets in terms of empowerment, entitlement, enhancement, enrichment and enlightenment.

India's vision of social transformation is not a static condition, but a dynamic process, with a universal, humanistic canvas, reflecting Jennifer Miller's (of the British Museum) observation that "the lofty, holistic and all inclusive vision of the sages of ancient India was cosmic, not just global".

It is not surprising that the International Liberal Manifesto (April 1947) echos the Indian concept of *"Vasudaiva Kutumbakam"* the universal family of man thus : "Liberty and individual responsibility are the foundations of civilised society; that the state is only the instrument of the citizens it serves; that any action of the state must respect the principles of separation of powers, that justice requires that in all criminal prosecution the accused shall enjoy the right to a speedy and public trial, and to a fair verdict free from any political influence; that state control of the economy and private monopolies both threaten political liberty; that rights and duties go together, that every citizen has a moral responsibility to others in society; and that a peaceful world can only be built upon respect for these principles and upon co-operation among democratic societies". India's vision of social transformation is global i.e., universal. Dr. Radhakrishnan pinpointed the challenge of change facing the leaders of India thus : "That future is not one of ease or resting but of incessant striving so that we might fulfil the pledges we have so often taken and the one we shall take today. The service of India means the services of millions who suffer. It means the ending of poverty and ignorance and disease and inequality of opportunity. The ambition of the greatest man of our generation has been to wipe every tear from every eye. That may be beyond us; but as long as there are tears and suffering, so long our work will not be over". [24]

A vision represents the ability to see beyond the present; an ability to map out the future, beyond decades and centuries of dynamic change. The vision of India was holistic and indivisible. In the evolutionary perspective of Indian civilisation and culture. *Abhyudaya* i.e., progress is a concept that can't be measured merely in quantitative terms such as standard of living or gross national product. The vision of India that the Constitution carved out focussed on the quality of life of every citizen, human development in the aggregate. Liberal democracy is a process of enhancement of citizens' freedom, human rights, rule of law, and free and fair elections, of religious belief, expression, association and the like. The vision of India as reflected in the

Constitution encompassed the political, the economic and the social processes as concurrent, democracy, development and governance as interdependent. The translation of such a vision warrants a 'mission-mode' of governance, a process far more focussed and dedicated than good governance.

References

1. Constituent Assembly Debates, Official Report, New Delhi, Government of India Press, Vol. IX No. 2 (2-9 Aug. 1949) P. 177.
2. The Constitution and the Constituent Assembly : Task before the Constituent Assembly, Inaugural Address, New Delhi, Govt. of India, Dr. Sachchidananda Sinha (Provisional Chairman), Dec. 1946, p. 6.
3. Dr. Rajendra Prasad, The Constitution and the Constituent Assembly Task before the Constituent Assembly Dr. Rajendra Prasad, December 11, 1946, pp. 10 – 11.
4. The Constitution and the Constituent Assembly; Salient features of the Constituent Assembly; Reply to Critics; Alladi Krishnaswami Ayyar, November 8, 1948, p. 132.
5. O.V. Alagesan Ibid 1948 p. 148.
6. The Constitution and the Constituent Assembly; Objectives Resolution; Significance of the Objectives; Dr. S. Radhakrishnan; January 20, 1947, p. 32.
7. The Constitution and the Constituent Assembly; Salient features of the Constitution; Important characteristics of the Constitution ; Alladi Krishnaswmi Ayyar, November 23, 1949, p. 162.
8. The Constitution and the Constituent Assembly; Salient features of the Constitution ;Achievements of the Constituent Assembly; M Ananthasayanam Ayyangar, November 18, 1949, p. 150.
9. The Constitution and Constituent Assembly; Salient features of the Constitution; Alladi Krishnaswmi Ayyar, November 8, 1948, p. 136.

10. The Constitution and Constituent Assembly; Objectives Resolution; Significance of the Objectives; Dr. S. Radhakrishna, January 20, 1947, p. 33.
11. The Constitution and Constituent Assembly; Salient features of the Constitution; The Draft Constitution; Dr. B.R. Ambedkar, November 4, 1948, p. 122.
12. The Constitution and Constituent Assembly; Salient features of the Constitution; Jawaharlal Nehru, November 8, 1948, pp. 134.
13. Granville Austin; The Indian Constitution : Cornerstone of a Nation, Clarendon Press, Oxford 1966, p. 9.
14. Jawaharlal Nehru; The Objectives Resolution, Constituent Assembly Debates; 13 Dec. 1946 p. 57.
15. The Constitution and the Constituent Assembly; Salient features of the Constitution; Merits of the Resolution; Alladi Krishnaswmi Ayyar, December 19, 1946, p. 26.
16. The Constitution and the Constituent Assembly; Salient features of the Constitution; Reply to the Debate; Syed Muhammad Saadulla, November 9, 1948 p. 142.
17. The Constitution and the Constituent Assembly; Salient features of the Constitution; Dedication to tasks ahead; Dr. Rajendra Prasad, August 15, 1947, p. 67.
18. The Constitution and the Constituent Assembly; Salient features of the Constitution; Achievements of the Constituent Assembly; M Ananthasayanam Ayyangar, November 18, 1949, p. 153.
19. Alladi Krishnaswmi Ayyar, November 18, 1949, p. 154.
20. The Constitution and the Constituent Assembly; Salient features of the Constitution; The Draft Constitution; Dr. B.R. Ambedkar, November 4, 1948, p. 119.
21. *Ibid,* p. 120.
22. The Constitution and the Constituent Assembly; Objectives Resolution; Reply to the Debates; Jawaharlal Nehru, January 22, 1947, p. 34.
23. S M Mehta, A commentary of Indian Constitutional law, 2nd ed. Deep and Deep Publications, New Delhi, 1990 p. 215.
24. Dr. S. Radhakrishna, *ibid* p. 60.

3

MISSION MODE

The Challenge

Actions pursued with (a) clarity of goals, supported by (b) adequate and appropriate skills / capability to perform, (c) dedication (positive values and attitudes) and (d) discipline (conviction, commitment) lead to a motivational drive to achieve a set of quantitative and qualitative targets/results. All these elements, together, can contribute to a mission-mode of action, at the level of individuals, institutions as well as large communities including nation-states and global organisations. This was best illustrated in the case of India's freedom movement. Swaraj was the mission, a whole generation was drawn into the movement, contributing to its fulfilment. That was mobilisation in the true sense of the term.

Bhagavad Gita went one step further in refining dedication : "*Karmanyevadhi Karasya*' - - *ma* - - *Phaleshu*" – perform duty with dedication without worrying about results. The legendary Arjuna was quoted in the Mahabharata that he could see only the eye of the bird, and nothing else, as he aimed his arrow, while mastering the art of archery. We have several illustrations of 'mission-mode' of action within the Indian society. It was Mahatma Gandhi who observed: "the lives of millions of Indians constitute my politics".

We had adopted a 'mission-mode' in our pursuit of political freedom, *Swaraj* and succeeded. We had repeated the mission-mode in designing our Constitution, clarifying our national aims and goals, modes of democracy, development and design for governance, aimed at *Sampoorna Swaraj* – as the substance of *Swaraj*. "Our Constitution marked the culmination and consummation of our glorious epic struggle for freedom, reflecting the lofty *ideals* and *values* that *inspired* the historic crusade, and enshrined the cherished *goals* and *objectives* that "we the people of India" have set for ourselves, for the achievement of which we have to dedicate ourselves and strive utmost with all our hearts and conscience".[1]

The Constitution of India was designed in a manner as to translate the vision – a mission-mode of governance; it represents a fine document of state-craft. Five cardinal elements of the Constitution shape this mission-mode : (i) a large network of organisations crafted with commonality of objectives and complementarity of roles, every single unit important in its own place; (ii) elected representatives (and political parties) as the prime-movers, the engines of the Republic; (iii) appointed functionaries as (a) the managers, of development/ change, with a non-partisan character, and (b) of the Justice system, as the 'umpires', with their independence fully safeguarded; (iv) sovereignty and thus centrality of "we the people", participating through (a) expression of their will, and securing compliance through the electoral process, and (b) decentralised structures of governance, constantly promoting and sustaining legitimacy of democratic social transformation; and (v) mission-technology, the process of focussed management that facilitates the fulfilment of the mission. If the letter of the Constitution provides clarity to the mission, it is the mission-mode that actualises the processes of democracy, development and governance, and thus lends nourishment and credibility to the spirit of the Constitution.

A unified vision, shared concerns, consensualism, and a spirit of comeradery characterised the working of the Consembly while harmonising and resolving even vexatious issues such as the division of powers between the states and the Centre. "A committee was appointed and the premiers of provinces (Prime Ministers, as they were known, then) who came before it gladly yielded wherever it was found necessary and thus strengthened the Centre. Even in the field of industry and commerce whenever Parliament (Consembly) found it necessary that in the public interest of India as a whole, a particular industry should be regulated by the central legislature it was granted in the interest of the country as a whole",[2] avers Ananthasayanam Ayyangar, reflecting on the salient characteristics of the working of the Consembly. The same spirit of consensualism prevailed while considering the otherwise contentious issue of language. Ananthasayanam Ayyangar refers to the question of language over which "we thought there will be much controversy at one stage. three or four times we met outside the House and also inside and ultimately we have resolved the question harmoniously. Hindi has been accepted as the *lingua franca* or the official language of India. These are all matters each one of which, for its solution, would have taken many months, if not years. We have resolved them all in the short period of time at our disposal".[3]

Referring to the serious complaint that there is too much of centralisation and that the states have been reduced to municipalities, Dr. Ambedkar clarified that this view is not only an exaggeration, but also founded on a misunderstanding of what exactly the Constitution contrives to do. Dr. Ambedkar argued that "as to the relation between the Centre and the states, it is necessary to bear in mind the fundamental principles on which it rests. The basic principle of federalism is that the legislative and executive authority is partitioned between the Centre and the states not by any law to be made by the Centre, but by the Constitution itself. This is what the Constitution does. The states under our Constitution are in no way dependant upon the Centre for their legislative or executive authority. The Centre and the states are coequal in this matter".[4] Each unit is important in its own place. While admitting the charge that the centre has been given the power to override the states, Dr. Ambedkar pleaded that certain considerations must be borne in mind, that the use and operation of "these overriding powers are expressly confined to emergencies only", adding, "could we avoid giving overriding powers to the Centre when an emergency has arisen? Those who do not admit the justification for such overriding powers to the Centre even in an emergency, do not seem to have a clear idea of the problem which lies at the root of the matter".[5] The Constitutional 'vision' has integrated and harmonised both the ends and means of our democratic republic. The process of Mission-mode can be seen as embedded within the framework of the Constitution of India : (1) the Mission (2) the network of instrumentalities, (3) the roles assigned to the people manning different instrumentalities / institutions and (4) the processes of management. The roles assigned to the people have been grouped into three distinctive clusters viz. (a) the elected representatives manning the political institutions as the prime-movers, (b) those who are appointed to manage the diverse range of institutions of governance, and (c) the role and place of the demos themselves participating as the citizens.

3.1. The Mission Mode

Participation both as a means as well as an end objective of democratic sustainable development, through good governance constitutes the mission set out by the Constitution. The design parameters for the mission are thus set by the Constitution, against which the 'performance' values can be measured so as to appreciate the fulfilment of the mission, and if there are deviations, the causes and consequences thereof so as to learn from the shortfall, and to provide course correction. It is a fascinating and challenging exercise to identify the design parameters and factors of shortfall or deviation. It was stated at the outset that this exploration is illustrative rather than empirical, methological more than substantial. Inorder to appreciate the nuances and challenge of democratic development and good governance, it would be appropriate and necessary to take an overview of (a) the dimensions and dynamics of social change, which is inherent, spontaneous and eternal in [every society], and development which is directed social change.

It is axiomatic to state that 'change' is the only 'constant' in human society. Consequently social institutions – be it a family, a corporate organisation or the institutions of state have to take cognizance of social change and attune as well as adjust constantly, to the process of change in the society. A series of questions emerge especially for the consideration of leadership of organisations. Some of the important questions are : (1) what is the framework for the analysis and appraisal of organisations – their performance? (2) How to identify the elements of social change? What are their dimensions and dynamics? (3) What is the nature of interaction between the society, its process of change, and organisations, which operate within the society? Is that reciprocal or unidirectional? and (4) what are the parameters for, and modus of management of change? These and similar issues bring to the fore a set of conceptual and ideological facets as well as the strategies and styles of management of change. A detailed, empirical and analytical exercise with reference to any specific society and its organisations would, of course, be fascinating and insightful.

Change takes place in a variety of ways, in all societies and at all times, though the pace varies. Change can be seen from many an angle. Broadly, change can be seen in terms of three sets (a) values, (b) socio-economic conditions, and (c) technological factors. Change process forms a continuum in terms of the past, the present and the future. Both evolutionary and revolutionary processes of change fit into this continuum. An overview of the interface between the factors and dynamics of social change is indicated in Illustration 3.1. For a detailed discussion see ref (6).

The process of change in any society takes place as a continuum; past situation merges with the present reality, which in turn sets the trend for and fuses with the future. It is the futuristic aspirations, ideals and vision of people that operate as the beacon light for organisational change management.

In no society and at no point of time the diverse factors of change are in fusion with each other, nor do they contribute to change at the same pace; there is a constant inter play, and they are always in a sate of flux. This is why, at any given point of time, there is a wide variation between groups within any society. That is why the factors of change generate and represent a maze of competing and conflicting values,

ILLUSTRATION 3.1
PROCESS OF SOCIAL CHANGE
Dimensions, Dynamics, Mangament

SOCIAL CHANGE		
Process of change	Past Present Future	Continuum
Factors of change Ideological Socio-economic Technological	Situation Reality Vision Competing / Conflicting Values Interests Identities	Vision Ideals Social transformation

Complex Demands ▶ Multiplicity of Organizations

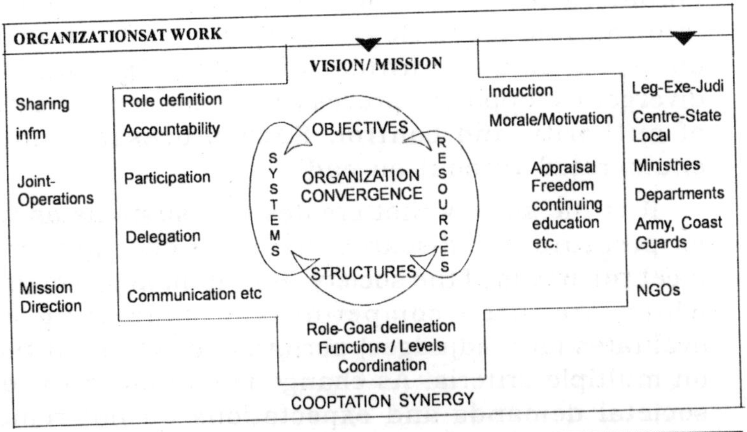

DYNAMIC MODE			
Redefine	Redesign	Monitor	Appraise
Refine objectives Prioritize Set performance- Standards SWOT	Role – Goal clarity Coordination Cooptation Design / Induct Mgt. Information Systems	Consumer / Citizen Satisfaction Quality of service Evaluate performance Feed back	Productivity espirit de corps Training Needs Analysis Change needs

TOWARDS EXCELLENCE : INTEGRATE TRG, RES & ORG. DEV.		
Scan / Forecast environment Monitor Social change Role alignments Mark policy issues Evaluation of performance	Attune values / attitudes Upgrade knowledge / skills Formulate agenda and strategies for change Develop Internal change agents	Professionalization Negotiate / shape policy Secure external inputs Protect from external threats Initiate action for change

interests and identities. It is the role of political process in society, and leadership of organisations to harmonise these competing and conflicting factors with reference to the long-term ideals and vision of the society. This process can be illustrated with reference to (a) freedom movement leading to democratisation (with emphasis on liberty and freedom); (b) the Indian Constitution promising the translation of human rights (political, economic, social and cultural) into a reality; and (c) globalisation and liberalisation of economies; information technology initiating 'revolutionary' changes in communication, participation and divergently opposite process such as centralisation of authority and control. Such processes can be enumerated without an end.

It is the society that creates and sustains as well as pressures or discards organisations inorder to meet the needs of the society. But, it makes demands, which are often competing and conflicting and evaluates (and adjudges) performance of institutions on multiple criteria. As change is eternal in society, societal demands and expectations do not remain static, but, gradually evolve and often change abruptly or violently. Thus, organisations have to constantly monitor (a) the process of social change, (b) the emerging and changing trends and demands (c) harmonise the competing and conflicting demands, into organisational objectives; and (d) prepare the organisation to achieve or contribute to such objectives. The more efficient organisations do not wait for the society to make fresh demands in tune with the social change, but keep a constant watch over emerging change and prepare in advance to meet the demands in a more 'proactive' manner. There is also the category of organisations (especially in the competitive corporate sector) that generate conditions of change and convert them into markets for profits.

The time lag between fresh demand and organisational response has to be reduced, if not eliminated. It is often observed that due to this lag, organisations continuously fight yesterday's problems, fail to cope with today's situation, and are blissfully unaware of tomorrow's emerging challenges. Organisations process the societal demands, reconcile the competing and conflicting demands, prioritise them and prepare the organisations in good time to perform. There are organisations, which are effective but not efficient and vice-versa. Performance and productivity depend upon both external effectiveness (meeting the sdemands) and internal efficiency (mode of meeting the demands).

Three responses on the part of organisations assume critical significance in the management of their interface with the society i.e., the environment of which they are a part and within which they have to operate. First, the society – almost all the societies and at all the times – generates contradictory and conflicting demands. Efficient organisations facilitate and help themselves with a precise definition of their role so as to reduce, demand-response gap, and minimise role-goal conflict. It is a funciton of the organisational leadership. Second, (emerging from the logic of the first), no professional orgnaisation 'takes' 'policy' as 'given' but assumes an active role in 'shaping' policy so as to ensure role-goal clarity without ambiguity or conflict. The degree of role clarity and image of organisational leadership are directly and positively correlated. Third, all organisations contribute to the shaping of future vision of the society of which they are a part, and sponetaneously contribute towards the fulfilment of such a vision. Futurological explorations, sketching a vision of the future, and translation of such a vision into a reality represent the most creative opportunities and a constant challenge to any organisation. It is such an understanding that helps shaping the organisational responses, promoting an image of creativity.

The organisational responses to the constant process of social change, and societal demands can be seen as falling into four processes which can be labelled as (a) Clarity over the Organisational Objectives, (b) Reengineering/fine-tuning the organisation so as to be able to meet the changing needs and objectives, (c) designing and induction of support systems, as management aids, and finally, the most critical one viz., (d) Human Resources Development and Management.

Organisational Effectiveness

Any organisation – be it a production or service, public or private, profit or non-profit – can be apprised in terms of (a) 'effectiveness' in the clarity, and translation of its objectives-goals-results, and (b) internal 'efficiency' in the organisation of its roles and relations, and generation and utilisation of resources, human, financial and material.

Organisational effectiveness is related to the recognition, formulation and crystalisation of objectives, which are derived from the social (socio-economic-political) environment. Indeed, objectives of any organizaton as set out by the environment in the form of 'expectations' of diverse stake-holders of the organiLaiton. There is always wide-range of 'interest groups', and an equally wide-range of 'interests'. Harmonisation of these wide-range of competing and conflicting interests constitutes an integral part of formulation of the "MISSION" of any organisation. At the level of a nation it is for the national leadership to formulate the national mission by harmonising divergent and occasionally conflicting interests. That is the prime function opf democratic leadership. Similarly, it is for the organisational leaders to recognise the wide-ranging expectations, and reconcile, harmonise and prioritise them. What is more, since no social environment remains stagnant but undergoes constant changes, harmonising divergent and conflicting interests is a constant function of organisational leadership.

In order to ensure organisational effectiveness, on a continuing basis, an 'environmental watch' or scanning is essential to find out the changing expectations and fine-tune the organisational objectives. It is the responsibility of organisational leadership not only to respond, but to forecast 'futuristic' demands, negotiate with the society and prepare in good time, their organisations to meet those futuristic demands. Where this does not happen, organisations lend to lose their creditability, disuse, misuse and abuse set in, leading to their 'demise', since society rejects them as non-performing and as irrelevant. Institutions are not only marginalised and rejected, societies also indulge in 'mercy-killing' of organisations that are out-of-tune with the changing times. Practices such as earlier 'nationalisation' and contemporary privatisation, disinvestment, talk of privatisation of (some aspects of) policing represent some of he glaring examples. Social safety net, golden hand-shake and the like measures represent the palliatives to make mercy killing less painful. Society adopts diverse modes in either marginalising or appreciating the 'networth' of an organisation, by creating collateral institutions to operate in a parallel or complementary manner with the pre-existing ones.

The internal process of any organisation can be seen, broadly, in terms of (a) setting objectives, (b) fine-tuning the structures, (c) designing and inducting support systems, and the all important (d) human resources development and management.

(a) Objectives

Constant attunement of objectives (including prioritisation) is only the starting point for promoting institutional efficiency.

(b) Structures

Clarity and crystallisation of objectives and converting them into measurable results and goals leads to an analysis of the organisational structures (vertical and horizontal units, and linkages between them; functional specialisation; decision making processes; centralisation-decentralisation; participative processes, etc.) on the one hand, and an assessment of their adequacy, appropriateness as well as areas where changes (reforms) are essential, on the other.

(c) Systems

Any organisational-structure, inorder to fructify its objectives, has to be supported by adequate and appropriately designed systems of management. Small and informal organisations operate on the basis of informal systems. But large, complex and formal organisations have to be supported by explicitly stated, uniformly understood formal systems. It is easy to design and install, for example, a police communication network. But, it can contribute to either centralisation of authority or can promote decentralisation. Systems are not synonymous with philosophy of management. That is why, the debate often assumes the form of 'man versus system' in the management of organizatons. The nature and degree of knowledge, skills, values of the people and clarity of role and 'commitment' to the objectives are critical to the management of internal efficiencies, Management of change always starts with people.

Excellence in performance

Where the society at large (at the level of communities, nations on an universal basis) is dynamic, even to stay where they are, in terms of performance, organisations have to keep running, organisational management has to be dynamic in order to attain and maintain a level of excellence on a continuing basis. There are four processes that help organisations retain dynamism and promote excellence in performance. These can be identified as (a) **Redefine** the role and objectives, (b) **Redesign** (re-engineer) the structure, (c) **Monitor** the citizen (consumer) orientation, and concerns for quality and cost, and (d) **Appraise** the organisational performance regularly.

(a) Redefine the role and objectives in tune with the changes taking place in the society and the complex (and conflicting) demands made by the society. The police organisations in India today are subjected to partisan influences. Just as the river Ganga cannot be blamed for its pollution, police need not accept the blame. In order to be able to do that, police have to explore ways and means of containing the pollution, negotiate with the polity in setting objectives and priorities for the police (i.e. create and cultivate a role in shaping policy, as a professional organisation), and set out explicit performance standards by which police must be judged. An exercise in the analysis of internal strengths, weaknesses, as well as extrnal opportunities and threats (SWOT) should be neither esoteric nor occasional but a constant process, for it helps like a preventive check-up of the status of organisational health, rather than remedial treatment.

(b) Redesign (re-engineer) the organisation, on a continuing basis in tune with the changing (expanding / contracting) role, objectives and performance standards set out. Design changes would also encompass the processes of cooptation (joint operations, command and control) and various management support processes such as decentralisation and community participation. Redesigning acquires significance in promoting role-goal clarify and congruence. Redefinition and Redesign help integrate and harmonise the external changes and the consequential internal change management.

(c) Monitoring the citizen / consumer satisfaction / (dissatisfaction) alongwith quality, cost and time parameters constitutes the third dimension of management for promoting excellence in performance. They provide the bench-mark for measuring the degree and direction of either excellence or slipp age in performance warranting diverse remedial measures. Stake-holder interactions would help setting performance standards and would help meet the performance standards set, and in the formulation of plans for Organisational Development. It makes a significant difference if the administration looks at problems of people as the feed back, rather than handling them as 'grievances'.

It is easier to map out the dimensions and dynamics of social change / development. The fascinating challenge emerges when we try to map out the analytical elements of a complex society, like India which is pursuing the path of development with democracy as a means as well as an end objective. Added to that complexity is the fact that the boundaries of nation-states have started melting towards the end of 20th century in such a manner that nation-states stand exposed to the external factors, as much if not more than the internal dynamics. The process of globalisation and the multiplicity of powerful factors today threaten the sovereign status of nation-states, especially of the newly independent, emerging democracies. The stresses and strains that the nation- states are subjected to are indicated in Illustration 3.2.

Illustration 3.2

SYNCHRONISATION – DISSONANCE – ENERVATION OF THE STATE AS A SYSTEM

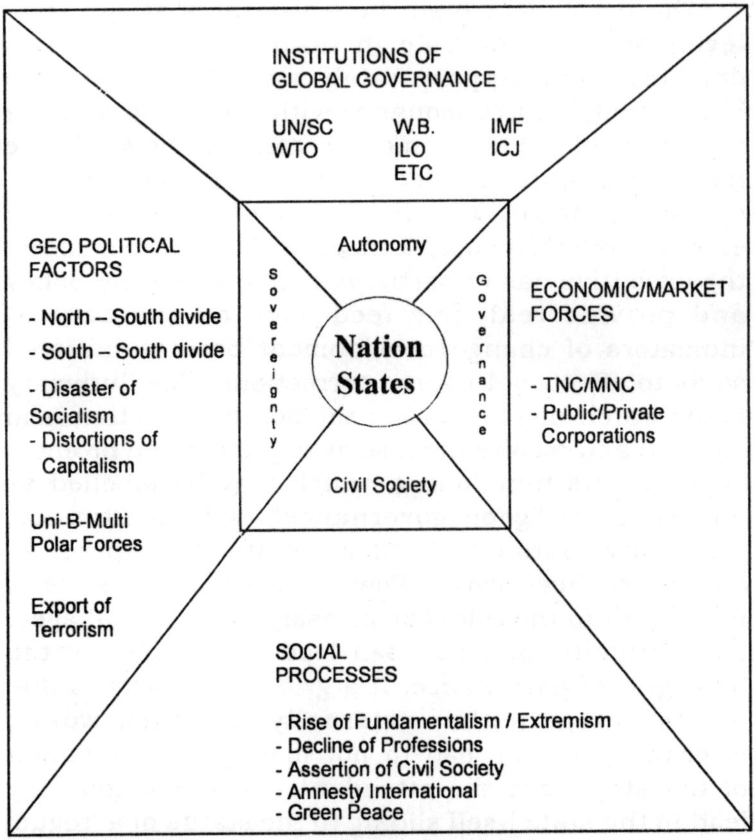

Mission mode of governance warrants synchronisation of the nation-state as a system, having a large number of sub-systems, and a large number of instruments with diverse but complementary functions. Synchronisation is a vital prerequisite for the system to be able to meet the performance parameters and values, and for the fulfilment of the mission. Small, seemingly insignificant slips in the process of synchronisation can prove disastrous to the mission itself as demonstrated in the U.S. space mission 'challenger' (2003) seconds before the touch down.

The Parliament (and the legislatures at the state level) have a vital role in taking note of issues, defining them appropriately and resolving them harmoniously in consonance with the vision and the objectives of the mission of governance. The executive has to translate the decisions into actions with an eye on productivity (internal efficiencies and external effectiveness) and time-frame. Even more, the executive has to participate in shaping the policy and provide real-time feed-back on the contra-indicators of change/development process initiated so as to effect mid-course corrections. The Judiciary is the watch-dog to monitor the points of friction (and conflict) and resolve them so as to protect and promote synchronous functioning, which may be labelled as an aspect of "good governance" (with legitimacy, credibility, autonomy and accountability operating as a four-wheel drive). 'Power' vested in the state is in relation to the roles/tasks assigned. Any leakages, short-cricuits, or surge can lead to a failure of the total grid of governance. If a grid failure occurs due to a sabotage (either externally, or much worse, internally), it can lead to not merely an enervation of the state, but the attendant chain reaction may lead to the state itself sliding to the status of a 'rogue' state or a 'failed' state. The global dialogue on development during the closing decade of the 20th century revealed that in many an instance the state itself was found to be the problem, the cause of distortions in the processes of 'management' and 'development'.

Some of the contemporary issues of national debate in India reveal 'deflection' in the focus and 'dissonance' in the modus of management with the consequence that issues that ought to be addressed by the Parliament are allowed, to be taken to the streets. On many an occasion, the very definition of issues has been distorted. Contemporary debate over issues such as (a) reservation for women in the legislature, (b) fixed-terms for legislatures (c) simultaneous polls for the parliament as well as state legislatures, (d) Supreme Court having to direct the executive wing in matters that the executive on its own ought to have done, (e) use and abuse of police to meet partisan ends, (f) river waters, and a host of others reveal a serious distortion of issues leading to anarchic conditions not conducive to the fulfilment of the vision.

3.2. Mission Mode : Overarching Parameters

Article 1 of the draft constitution referred to India as "a union of states', over which there was an intense debate in terms of union vis-à-vis federation of states. Dr. Ambedkar explained as to why the Drafting Committee has used the expression : "to make it clear that though India was to be a federation, the federation was not the result of an agreement by the states to join in a federation and that the federation not being the result of an agreement, no state has the right to secede from it. The federation is a union because it is indestructible. Though the country and the people may be divided into different states for convenience of administration, the country is one integral whole, its people a single people living under a single imperium derived from a single source. The Drafting Committee thought that it was better to make it clear at the outset rather than to leave it to speculations or to dispute".[7] The draft constitution, in the words of Dr. Ambedkar, "can be both unitary as well as federal according to the requirements of time and circumstances. In normal times, it is framed to work as a federal system. But in times of war it is so designed as to make it work as though it was a unitary system".[8]

The Constitution provided for a dual polity with a single citizenship, the Indian citizenship. Every Indian has the same rights of citizenship, irrespective of place of birth or domicile. The means adopted by the draft constitution to promote the spirit of federalism are three : (a) a single judiciary, (b) uniformity in fundamental laws, civil and criminal, and (c) common all India civil service. Reflecting on the necessity to include such administrative details in the Constitution, Dr. Ambedkar cites Grote, the historian of Greece, who said : "the diffusion of constitutional morality not merely among the majority of any community but throughout the whole, is the indispensable condition of a government at once free and peaceful; since even any powerful and obstinate minority may render the working of a free institution impracticable, without being strong enough to conquer ascendancy for themselves".[9] The very concept of federalism implies mutuality and commonality. These two characteristics of federalism can be promoted by (a) a process of complementarity in place of exclusivist, much less confrontationist, dispositions, (b) provision of adequate and appropriate institutional mechanisms to promote harmony, (c) cultivation of conventions rather than legislated norms, (d) decentralisation in a manner as to promote citizen participation, and a sense of belonging, (e) judicial creativity inorder to maintain the process on an even keel, even in the face of possible friction, and (f) bringing the political parties within the purview of constitutional status and accountability. Federalism, by the very definition, is a relationship of mutuality between units. Such a structure can be operated only on a premise that "conflicts will occur and that they can always be resolved". Such a disposition alone can promote and sustain an organic federalism – bonds between the units, and a strong nation.

Federalism has to be seen as a factor not only between the centre and the states, but also as between the units. In the Indian context, inter-state relations have emerged as a major issue more than and more frequently than the centre-state relations. Issues of natural resources have not been explored as national issues but pursued as inter-state disputes. Inter-State issues have been construed and converted into centre-state problems and disputes. Issues of national security have been distorted by pursuing them in terms of autonomy of states in the context of a national debate on the need for a federal law on national security. Federal issues and policies were often discussed and decided on the basis of political / party equations obtaining as between the Centre and the states.

Public discourse on the constitutional scheme of 'roles and relations' between the Centre and the states has been distorted in terms of a "strong centre versus strong states" as the debate was cast in the framework of political parties, and political power. Consequently, their positions and dispositions got shifted based on their fluctuating fortunes at the husting, the emergence of regional parties, and the dynamics, constraints and compromises of coalitions. The national concerns for a 'strong nation' were often lost sight of, and even given up in the struggle for power, polarised in terms of a 'strong centre' versus 'strong states' as indicated in Illustration 3.3.

ILLUSTRATION 3.3
PATTERNS OF CENTRE-STATE RELATIONS

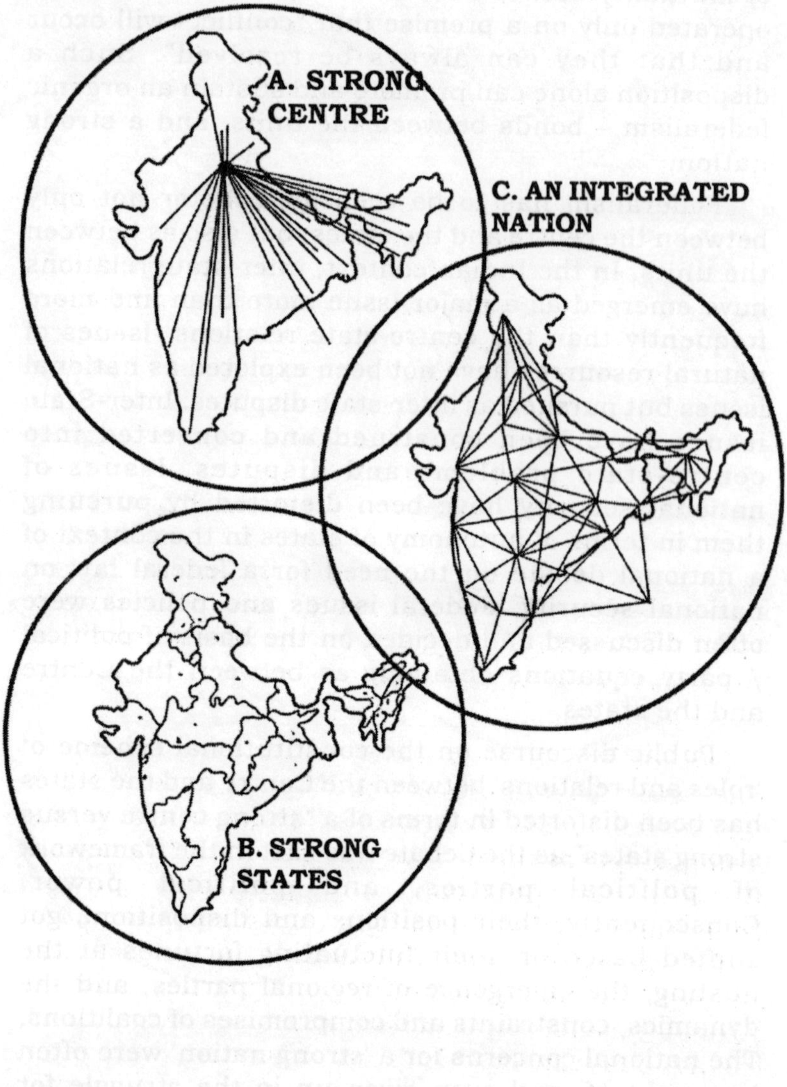

The features of centralisation in the Indian polity emerged from the circumstances under which the Constitution was made. The founding fathers were concerned about the unity and integrity of the nation at a time of the partition and the communal holocaust, the challenge of integration of princely states, the threat of the Nizam declaring independence, and secessionist movements looming large. The arguments with which Dr. Ambedkar prevailed upon the Constituent Assembly to approve the distribution of powers are worth quoting : "The Constitution establishes a dual polity with the union at the Centre and the states at the periphery, each endowed with sovereign power to be exercised in the field assigned to them respectively by the Constitution. The union is not a league of states, united in a loose relationship, nor are the states the agencies of the union, deriving powers from it. Both the union and the states are created by the Constitution, Both derive their respective authority from the Constitution. The one is not subordinated to the other in its own field; the authority of one is coordinate with that of the other". Rebutting the argument that the states have been reduced to municipalities, Dr. Ambedkar argued that it is "wrong to say that the states have been placed under the centre. The center cannot by its own will alter the boundary of this partition. Nor can the Judiciary"[10].

NETWORK OF UNITS AND TIERS

An overview of the network of institutional units on the horizontal plane and tiers on the vertical plane is presented briefly though, in Illustration 3.4. The process of constitutionally assigned complementarity of roles and commonality of the objectives can be achieved only through a process of horizontal cooptation and vertical integration. The two sides of the coin of democracy viz. decentralisation and participation assign a critical role to the institutions of civil society inorder to fructify the constitutional parameters of democratic development and good governance.

The constitutional design has also provided for a set of overarching norms to ensure the productive functioning of the various units and to shape their *inter-se* role-relationships. Some of these overarching normative parameters can be identified thus : (a) people as the source of the democratic imperium, (b) one nation, with its integrity and integration as of vital significance, (c) one citizenship with equal rights to all, (d) democratic character and ethos as a value imparting precedence to sanctity at electoral process over concerns such as freedom of expression, all of them oriented to strengthen the vision, and its pursuit on a mission mode.

Institutional complementarity is provided for so as to establish and sustain synchronisation of roles, goals and role-relationships. Synchronisation as in the case of ministers and civil servants, is a key process as the output of one unit becomes the input to other units. This fusion is designed inorder to ensure synergy and productivity[11] of the network as a whole and to contain diffusion and disarray. Similarly, autonomy (application of minds without fear or favour) has been provided for inorder to ensure accountable and transparent performance which is an essential prerequisite of good governance. Thus, the cardinal features of the structures of India's democratic polity are designed to promote decentralisation and participation in myriad ways. A major thrust of the role of the institutions of civil society is to protect and promote these two features. Any deficiency in regard to decentralisation and participation will lead to centralisation of structures, processes and authoritarian leadership, that could lead to disastrous

ILLUSTRATION 3.4

INDICATIVE NETWORK OF HORIZONTAL UNITS AND VERTICAL TIERS

THE REPUBLIC

CITIZENS

HORIZONTAL / VERTICAL	Constitutional/ Autonomous	EXECUTIVE	LEGISLATIVE	JUDICIAL	CONSTITUTIONAL/ QUASI-JUDICIAL	CONSULTATIVE/ ADVISORY
NATIONAL	C & AG UPSC RBI PRESS COUNCIL	PRESIDENT PRIME MINISTER PMO/CABINET PLG.COM MINISTRIES DEPARTMENTS FIELD UNITS	PARLIAMENT RAJYA SABHA LOK SABHA HOUSE COMMITTEES STANDING/ CONSULTATIVE/ JOINT/SELECT AD HOC JPC CONSULTATIVE	SUPREME COURT COMMISSIONS TRIBUNALS	ELECTION COMMISSION NHRC/SC & ST/ WOMEN/ MINORITIES COMMISSIONS FINANCE COMM.	PARLIA. COMMITTEES/ INTER-STATE COUNCIL NDC NATIONAL INTEGRATION COUNCIL EXPERT COMMITTEES/ COMMISSIONS
STATE		GOVERNOR CHIEF MINISTER	LEGISLATURE HOUSE COMMITTEES	HIGH COURTS TRIBUNALS	COMMISSIONERS OF INQUIRY FINANCE COMM.	ADVISORY COMMITTEES
ZILLA PARISHAD		CHAIRMAN COLLECTOR PRI FUNCTIONA-RIES	ZILLA PARISHAD GRAM SABHA	DISTRICT COURT	NYAYA PANCHAYATS	COMMITTEES
CIVIL SOCIETY	GONGOs	MEDIA	NGOs / CBOs	PROFESSIONS	TRADE UNIONS	TRADE ASSOCIATIONS

WE THE PEOPLE

CITIZENS

consequences in the form of citizen (the imperium) alienation, unrest, resistance and ultimately to socio-political upheaval. The process dynamics, as indicated in Illustration 3.5 prove as critical as the role definition/clarity of the units, and the over arching parameters of democracy.

ILLUSTRATION 3.5

STRUCTURERS OF DEMOCRATIC SOCIETY

Dynamics of Process

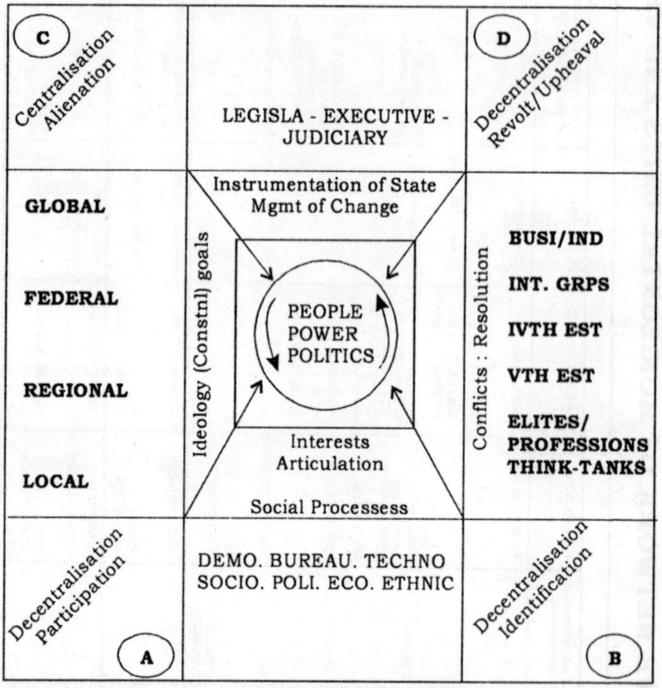

The hall-mark of any organisation or network of org anisations – be it a family (the smallest of human organisations) a business, educational, of governance, or of a coalition of 'sovereign' nations such as the United Nations – is the synergy created by the individual units working together. One of the finest examples where people of diverse values, interests and identities "organised" themselves with a common objective, and created a synergic effect is the freedom-movement of India. Where the individuals especially the "leadership" subsumes its personal or partisan agenda and identities, it contributes to synergy. Where individuals or groups pursue their roles, in isolation with a partisan agenda, organisational processes get dissipated, organisations get enervated, leading to a distorted debate such as "individual versus system". It is a function of leadership to transcend the partisan and thus create conditions of synergy. Where the leaders transgress the objectives of an organisation, the institution gets enervated.

Since India won "freedom", the wide network of political, social and institutions of governance are drowned in the "partisan", with its deleterious impact on the organisations. The leadership of all organisations missed the woods for the trees. Organisations are charaterised by a culture of 'conflict' internally, and 'confrontation' *inter-se*. Promoting synergy in all 'organised' activity is a function of leadership. Leadership is categorised as falling into two viz., 'lions' and 'foxes' on the basis of value-orientations, organisational commitment and courage of convictions, vis-a-vis partisan dispositions and pursuits, respectively. Experiments and experiences with in India, such as the Green Revolution, the Technology Missions and satellite launches have demonstrated these processes. Initiatives in regard to participative development, electoral reforms, and reform in the sphere of governance in India have proved abortive and reflected the quality of leadership. Experiences in the sphere of governance reveal a mismatch between promises vis-a-vis performance, on the one hand, and partisan pursuits and organisational objectives on the other. Analyses of experiences in the sphere of governance are couched in a language of conflict and confrontation: Center versus State, Ministers versus Civil Servants, legislature versus Judiciary, technocrat versus bureaucrat, generalist versus specialist, IPS versus IAS, and the like are expressions that characterise the *inter-se* adversary relations and the dominant organisational culture of the institutions of governance. Methods and manner of appointment of members of higher Judiciary to Commissions of Inquiry, and appointment of Chief Justices, soon after retirement to offices of profit often on extraneous considerations, show up as examples that have negated the image and efficacy of institutions of governance, contrary to the design parameters of complementarity and commonality of objectives, and constitutional ethos and culture.

A balanced distribution of political power has to be supported by an appropriate institutional framework and cultivation of organisational culture, contributing to an organic federalism. The National Development Council, the Inter-State Council, the Finance Commissions, and a host of other institutions such as the river-water tribunals have not been able to positively and adequately contribute to the dynamic process of a federal polity; instead, over a period of time they are showing signs of enervation and atrophy due to partisan political factors.

The Parliament of India constitutes, by design, the sovereign power-house with representatives exercising sovereign power of the people, as trustees. Parliament has been assigned the overarching role, *inter-alia,* of formulating and monitoring the implementation of policy, and of law. It is designed to articulate public opinion and to harmonise the competing and occasionally conflicting values, interests and identities and thus sustain the equilibrium of our pluralist democracy. This is an integral part of the process of maintaining continuity while promoting social change and development. With a multi-party system as a cardinal characteristic of our constitutional democracy, the 'Ruling' and the 'Opposition' parties are expected to participate in the grand debate within the normative frame of constitutional democracy, pluralist polity and political morality. Equally important is the nationalist spirit inspired by the freedom movement, and consensual agenda set out by the Constitution, by which all the functionaries of state, the legislative, the judicial and the executive, swear to protect, promote and defend.

The slide in the conduct of our Parliament and that of legislatures within a brief five decades, however is alarming and agonising. A slide in the performance of Parliament manifest in the form of low productivity or non-performance can be considered normally as an inadequacy. No organisation, of governance, business or of civil society, can attain and sustain 100 per cent efficiency, for all times. But, when any organisation reveals 'mal-function' it must be recognised as an 'emergency' situation. If a malfunctioning is detected but not attended to in good time, it would be an invitation to disaster. The nation has been a witness to such malfunctioning of the legislative, the Judicial and the executive instrumentalities of state on several occasions. Any neglect or delay in the 'corrective process would not merely 'burn-out' the instruments, but, the mission of demcoracy may be at stake. India had witnessed, and suffered such instance of malfunctioning earlier.

Peoples' mandate of the electoral system is polluted by the political parties, through the money, muscle, mafia factors operating in various combinations leading to defections, deception, abductions, hijacking of legislators et al. The saddest and the most critical slide is the corporatisation and marketisation of politics to an extent that the political parties and their activities represent the most dominant and powerful factors of corporate culture. Sale of party tickets to the highest bidder, foreclosing debate by the issue of whip, organised abstention from voting for extraneous (inconvenient) reasons, promulgation of constitutionally improper ordinances, are some of the politically immoral and democratically untenable practices that contribute to the distressing slide, reflecting such malfunctioning. The decline in the standards and quality of political leadership presents both the cause and effect of this malfunctioning. Within less than five decades the attributes of statesmanship have given way to deception and deceit in securing power and its misuse and abuse. Today, the qualities of 'Lions' of yester years are displaced by those of the 'Foxes'. The craving and vulgar display of 'privileges' totally unrelated to their functional efficacy as legislators, and betrayal of 'trust' reposed in them by the people as their 'representatives', generation of conflict in the polity as a means to secure and retain power, at any cost, and such other practices have contributed to the malignancy of the political process in the body politic of India. 'Biharisation' of the Indian polity is the consequence of the malfunctioning. Indian Parliament has reduced democracy as a number game, as if numbers is all about democracy. There was the exceptional exception of the late Indrajit Gupta who politely rejected medical treatment abroad offered by the government, by stating that he would not like to have anything that the ordinary citizens in India do not have.

The spillover of the political / legislative malfunctioning is manifesting in the form of toxic effluents and rapid spread of the malignancy. Illustratively, but not exhaustively, (1) generation of a culture of 'versus' 'conflict' and 'confrontation' within the political system and its practice within the legislatures, in place of Ruling and the Opposition both having a complementary task in sustaining parliamentary demcoracy; (2) violence of the worst order within the legislatures, leading to the 'law of the Marshals' if not marshal law; (3) practice of communal politics in an essentially secular polity; (4) converting social trauma (during instances such as disasters leading to loss of life and property) into political drama, and; (5) inducements such as Constituency Development Funds are all destructive of democracy. Of critical significance is the consequence of a mix-up in the exercise of power, creating short-circuits and flash-points.

The power-vacuum created by the Parliament / legislature by their own non-performance, and of malfunctioning has led to the other institutions stepping in to meet the constitutional exigencies. Such stepping in may be legitimate, or projected as a part of legitimisation. In the process, some institutions have tended to overreact, or even transgress their own boundaries of action. Some others had shown signs of usurping the powers of the Parliament, yet others had just twisted the tail of the Centre, under conditions of vulnerability. When the political process turns sick and malignant, it becomes vulnerable to external forces as well, in a variety of ways.

Rajya Sabha has been fashioned by the Constitution as a federal chamber, a chamber of elders but today it is reduced to a replica of *Lok Sabha.* Several Prime Ministers and political party leaders have reflected on the distortions in the changed character of Rajya Sabha and the futility of taking issues to *Rajya Sabha* because of the frozen dispositions based on the partisan political complexity, numerical composition, and the whip exercised by the parties.

The Constitution has clearly recognised that good governance – democratic, decentralised participative, responsive, responsible and accountable governance - with a challenging agenda of social transformation warrants a large and complex organisation. Provision of constitutional status to the institutions of *Panchayati Raj* (PRIs), appropriately referred to as the institutions of participative democracy and of self-governance, was considered by the Consembly. But action was deferred to the wisdom of the future leadership of the nation, due to their apprehension that the then prevailing social structure, especially in the rural communities, fractured by caste and other factors, might get hardened and perpetuated by the PRIs. Thus, with two constitutionally sanctified tiers viz. center and the states, India constituted an indestructible federation, but with alterable federal units. The Constitution itself defined their roles and distributed the legislative, financial, executive and judicial authority between the union and the states.

However, a series of amendments to the Constitution have significantly altered the role relations, and issues of vertical integration of the units of governance.[12] The issues and process of 'power-shift' have also loaded and distorted the role of judiciary. The process of vertical integration, and interface management as between the center and the states remained an unsettled agenda, and is growing in complexity, due to four major factors. These factors are (a) many of the nearly 100 amendments to the Constitution during the first five decades have tended to centralise power rather than decentralise; (b) the emergence of personality-centered, authoritarian leadership and fragmentation of the party system, emergence and coalition of regional parties to form the government at the Centre, (c) distortions in the appointment and constitutional role of Governors especially in recommending and imposing President's rule, dismissal of Chief Ministers instead of allowing the issue of majority status to be resolved by the legislature, and (d) provision of constitutional status to the *Panchayati Raj* Institutions (PRIs) as the third tier of decentralised, participative governance.

Before the emergence of PRIs as constitutional units, several national and the regional parties 'empowered' their respective cadres at the grass-root levels, while the bureaucratic structures and processes have hardened their centralised character. The *de jure* constitutional status of PRIs did not fructify into a *de facto* decentralisation of governance and participative development. PRIs remain the kitten of India's democracy, sandwiched between a la the two monkeys, the center and the states. In fact, a process of political 're-centralisation' has set in, even after the democratic decentralisation was mandated by the 73rd amendment. Indian democracy has ushered into the 21st century, with decentralisation and participation on hold.

The electoral process as the Basic Process of Power, has been vitiated consistently in an ever-increasing pattern, and remained uncorrected for long, leading to a chain of factors anamolies that have distorted the complementarity and the commonality of the mission mode of governance.

3.3. The Prime-Movers

Political process, in its pristine character, represents the elixir of a democratic society. The mission of political process is life-giving, life-nourishing and life-sustaining, constantly providing renewal, legitimacy and credibility to the processes of governance and social transformation. It was the mobilisation of people-men and women, young and the old, for political freedom, setting the agenda for building India as a modern nation, and as a model of democracy that marked the spirit of India's political resurgence as it was obtaining during the freedom movement. Father of the Nation observed that democracy does not mean imposition of the will of the majority on the minority but carrying the minority along. Indeed it was in this spirit and with the quintessentially democratic ethos that the Constitution was sculpted setting out the vision, the national agenda and institutional network for social reconstruction. Indian political ethos had ushered in democracy and constitutional consensualism. Indian democracy was not cast in terms of majority or minority of the people, but on an explicit rejection of it. The national agenda was carved out in an ethos of democratic consensualism – *Sarva Hita* and *Sarva Mata*. Peoples' participation was considered the best insurance to pursue the agenda of a revolutionary character through an "evolutionary" mode. But soon, very soon, there has been a radical transformation of the political leadership, process and political organisations from that of 'servants' of the people to one of 'masters' engaged, almost in exclusive terms, in the pursuit of power and pelf.

The consensual adoption of adult suffrage by the Consembly represents the hallmark of Indian democracy. It is based on a firm faith and conviction in the principles of parliamentary democracy. We haven't just adopted the Westminster model; we have consciously and carefully 'adapted' certain norms to suit our genius. The idea of direct elections on the basis of 'one-(wo)man - one-vote' emerged and came to be accepted, without much of a conflict of opinion, during the years of the freedom movement. A mute comment by a citizen in a remote village, the proverbially 'illiterate, poverty-stricken and ignorant' citizen, as to "why the chief ministers at the state level and the prime ministers at the national level should not be 'elected' by the legislators, just as the citizens elect their representatives, democratically through secret ballot, instead of by 'nomination' by the party high–command", speaks volumes on the validation of adult franchise and vitality of democracy in India. What can be the credentials of "some" educated property-holding citizens to deny "some others" the status and rights of citizenship of the Republic?; "some" formally educated to impose their decisions on some who are aware but not formally educated, in a country claiming to be a Republic? It has been demonstrated, conclusively and repeatedly, that compared to the more educated, it was the less-educated (semi-literate, and the illiterate) who by their participation, made democracy in India vibrant. And as for the fallacies and pitfalls that this Republic has suffered, it was not literacy that made the difference, but, myriad manifestations of corruption and some erosion of the system. Nani Palkhivala pinpointed the real variable as that : "tall men dominated the scene till India became a Republic, and pygmies who strut and fret their hour upon the stage"[13] have taken over since, whose focussed and near exclusive concern for 'power' made them lose sight of the vital issues of Indian democracy such as control of population growth, and responsibility with regard to primary education in tune with the injunction of Article 45 of the Constitution. The leadership seem to have neglected these two aspects deliberately as a strategy of (vote-catching) politics of power, leading to the disaster of a stunted national identity and a sense of freedom without responsibility.

People have recognised that the party system, operating outside the realm of the Constitution, calls for scrutiny inorder to promote its attunement to the democratic norms and ethic, in regard to aspects such as inner-party democracy, public accountability, and linkages between manifesto, mandate and performance. The ruling 'masters' have not found such an ethic conducive to the pursuit of power. It is a case of usurpation of power and debasement of democracy from within. The pursuit of political power, which is a legitimate and an essential prerequisite for the sustenance of democracy, is based not on the values of democracy, ideology or constitutional agenda but on securing power *per se*. Social fragmentation on the basis of caste, region and religion, reinforced by money and muscle power, have emerged as the dominant modes of the political parties in India today.

The vital role of the political system as one of the subsystems of the Constitutional Republic can be analysed with reference to three inseparably interrelated facets of democracy, development and governance. First the status, character and mode of functioning of the political parties would shape the internal management, and levels of efficacy of the party system. The management of the party system establishes and demonstrates its constitutional democratic character. The second dimension viz. the nature and quality of participation of the political parties in the elections determines the democratic legitimacy and credibility of the political system. Thirdly the level of effective performance, correlating the manifesto, popular mandate and its translation into action, establishes accountable and transparent process of governance. An overview of the five decades of constitutional democracy reveals critical deficiencies in (a) the character of the political party structures, the legitimacy and credibility of the electoral system and process, contributing to low levels of effectiveness of governance, reflected in terms of low level of accountability.

The political parties operate outside the constitutional frame, with a minimal statutory regulation; generate enormous funds not only to meet campaign expenses but also unaccounted corruption money both at the level of candidates and political parties and incur expenses on election campaign ten to hundred times the statutorily set limits over expenditure. The expenditure assumes the form of "investment" for profits that would accrue through abuse and misuse of office if elected. If "winnability" and ability to meet electoral expenses emerge as the two primary criteria in the choice of candidates, caste, religion and region provide the meat of campaign. The growing range of electoral malpractices, encompassing rigging and booth-capturing eliminate the chance of any honest citizen to be able to contest, much less get elected. The citizens have no voice in the selection of candidates, nor a true choice, excepting to desist from voting. Demos tend to withdraw from the democratic process, leading to those securing less than 50 per cent of vote getting elected.

The legitimacy and credibility of the electoral process is seriously eroded by the system of First Past and Post, and lack of accountability to the translation of manifesto into action on the ground. The greatest challenge to the legitimacy and credibility of the electoral process emerges from (a) an utter lack of commitment to the rules of the game on the part of the players, the political parties and the candidates, (b) the status, role, structure and systems of the Election Commission, (c) the constant encroachment of the Judiciary over the functions of another constitutional institutions viz., the Election Commission, and (d) growing necessity on the part of the Election Commission to show the 'red-card' and send the players who play foul, out of the game. The institution of independent observers operating as nominees of the Election Commission is found useful, but not adequate to control 'electoral frauds'. Preventive rather than remedial measures appear to be the urgent need inorder to contain and reverse the loss of legitimacy and credibility of the electoral system.

The effectiveness of the political system, especially with reference to its accountability and transparency, is diluted by factors such as; (a) the diffused vision of India (b) conflict as the prime mode, adopted by the parties, in the pursuit as well as management of power as against the consensual mode embedded in the Constitution and enjoined by it on the political subsystem; (c) distortion of the yard sticks of development and milestones of progress set by the Constitution; (d) the faulted processes of policy formulation, including the very definition of problems as a prerequisite for solution. Emerging from the distortions such as the conflict mode of management and deficiencies in the political processes, the conflict within the political subsystem is transmitted to the other subsystems of constitutional democratic governance viz. the legislative, the administrative and the judicial, leading to expansion of the conflict, short circuits and a critical level of adversary relations as between them. The more counter-productive consequence of political drag-factors is that the gravity of democracy is shifting from the polity, citizens are ending up without representation; the consequences could be grave in terms of institutionally induced conflict, disruption and anarchic conditions.

The span of the role of legislatures ranges from pursuing the vision of India, to managing the instrumentalities of State, including the judiciary, facilitating their autonomy and ensuring their legal and social accountability; providing an enabling environment for the role and efficacy of social forces and factors such as the media, non-governmental organisations and professional groups; and sustaining and enhancing the democratic methods and processes. As the national boundaries are melting due to factors such as (a) the ecological and environmental, (b) globalisation of economies the emergence of multi-lateral and global institutions, including trans-national corporations, and (c) ethnic and armed conflict, the role of legislatures is expanding and assuming higher levels of criticality. Given recognition to the intricate linkages among the political, the economic, and the social processes, and the institutional complementarity, the span of the role of legislatures in contemporary times encompasses all the facets of life of citizens from womb to tomb.

Disequilibrium is a universal characteristic of communities involved in rapid social change. But, containing and sustaining the degree of disequilibrium is a function of the democratic political process and mission-mode of governance. Thus, the performance of any legislature has to be analysed and validated from the stand-point of (a) internal efficiency, and (b) external effectiveness, in creating the desired impact on the society, especially in the Indian context, where there are two Houses of the national parliament and more than a score of state-level legislatures, some of them having Councils (Upper Houses).

(a) Internal Efficiency. Numerically large size, inadequate division of labour (committee structures), absence of specialisation in interests and participation (excepting in the form of consultative committees), and the party-whip are some of the characteristics that adversely affect the participation as well as the morale of the members of the legislatures. Due to these characteristics, the process of debate and discussion does not afford equal and adequate satisfaction in terms of (a) participation as a reward and incentive, (b) sense of involvement in shaping the policy, and (c) public recognition. Debates and discussions are conducted, in terms of "Ruling versus Opposition" with no concern for merit of arguments or consensus. Issues of public concern are not discussed in a creative atmosphere but, in a reactive, post-facto, fault-finding disposition. Due to this adversarial disposition democratic traditions and conventions are not built up. Issues such as the election of the Speaker, the umpiring of discussions and debates, and discipline fail to transcend party lines. On the other hand, partisan lines often get reinforced by the 'whip'. Since many important issues are discussed and sought to be resolved outside, the legislatures tend to get devalued. Political groups change their positions, at periodic intervals, from the Ruling to the Opposition and vice-versa, but without a change in their mutually adverse dispositions.

Legislative process is also vitiated by distortions in defining and setting up legislative agenda, and inadequate marshalling of data. Use of financial rather than physical targets of achievement makes debates fractious. In the absence of codification of privileges of legislators and legislatures, and mix up between the two, much time and energy are dissipated; there often is a mix-up of the privileges required for performing the legislative functions and financial and material benefits that have nothing to do with legislative responsibilities and performance.

The functioning of legislatures in India is characterised by one distinct attribute viz., legislators tend to demand and provide legislated norms, where there are stringent laws already in existence. The effort is not directed towards an examination of why the existing legislation and the law enforcing machinery have failed but the proneness is to make ever more stringent laws with the result that with regard to the same problem there are two or more different provisions of law. Legislation is substituted for problem-solving, with a naïve assumption and satisfaction as if the problem is resolved. If during the hundred years (1847-1947) before India secured political freedom there were about 400 pieces of legislation, in the first 40 years since Independence, Indian legislatures have enacted more than 4,000 pieces of legislation. India has become a legalistic and litigatious but by no means a 'rule of law', society. The legislative avalanche is attended by more administrators, more judges, and a docket explosion, resulting in Justice delayed in a manner that it is denied. Even administrators and members of the judiciary were found unaware of many laws they were supposed to be administering. India, perhaps, can be cited as the best (or worst) case of a country that adopted legislation as almost the only mechanism for the resolution of conflict in society.

(b) External Effectiveness. As a consequence of party organisations operating as mechanisms without concern for and an effort towards consensus in the legislative process, Indian society is getting more and more fragmented, contrary to the foundational values set out in the Preamble to the Constitution, and the Directive Principles of State Policy. Openness, creative and innovative interaction, and a problem-solving disposition are conspicuous by their absence.

Social transformation is not seen in terms of standards of living and quality of life of the community, but explained in terms of budgetary allocations. The performance of the executive branch entrusted with the task of implementation - in the role of change agents - and its performance and accountability are hardly evaluated by the legislatures. So is the case with justice delivery system which has not been given the attention it deserves.

Whenever and wherever there is a public outcry for reform and change in the administrative system – judicial, executive, and other quasi-judicial institutions – commissions are appointed (in the area of labour, police, judiciary, administration *et al*), and reform measures are reported, at a huge cost to the exchequer. There is hardly any review, much less follow-up action. Consequently, the democratic character of the legislative process and that of the society are vitiated. "In spite of having a national government responsible to legislatures elected on the adult franchise, the situation, which was never terribly good, has actually become worse".[14] While this was seen as one of the great contradictions in the Indian scene by an eminent administrator in 1967, it has only further deteriorated by 1992, as the nation was aspiring to enter into the 21st century. The Fulton Commission in England (1966-1968) began their report by saying : "The Home Civil Service today is still fundamentally the product of the 19th century of the Northcote-Travelyan Report (1854). The tasks it faces are those of the second half of the 20th century. This is what we have found, it is what we seek to remedy". The Indian administrative structure, a product of the 19th century (Lord Macaulay's Report : 1854) is bogged down with yesterday's structures and systems geared to an alien rule designed for 'subjects', with remote controls, and oriented to status quo. The legislatures have demonstrated neither conviction nor the inclination to democratise the systems. In such a situation, the legislative effort goes waste, at its worst it enables the parties and representatives to step into the colonial system of controls.

Productivity of a legislature can be measured in terms of (a) proper utilisation of available time (b) costs and benefits of legislative process both in absolute and comparative terms; (various large committees undertake extensive tours within and outside the country, but do not find time to attend to the 'schedule' of work; even worse, reports are not fed back into the legislatures), and (c) political-will leading to creativity and innovation in problem solving. In the face of declining productivity and escalating popular disenchantment about the performance of legislatures, the democratic system is heating up, adversely affecting productivity, as well as the process of democratic social transformation.

In the background of universal adult franchise, a positive factor is the increasing levels of the educational profile of the legislators. However, legislative support services, which are almost absent today, should be considered in the light of : (a) nature of recruitment and the profile of cadres of political parties; (b) profile of legislators; (c) adequacy of the educational system in meeting the demands of parliamentary democracy; (d) demands of nourishment for the political process compatible with democratic development; and (e) facilitating creative interaction between the political functionaries and the other professional groups, so as to promote enrichment of debate and professional ethos in politics. There is also a need for capability building (on a continuing basis), needed to perform the role: assigned for the promotion of a set of professional ethics, a code of conduct, and a culture of setting standards of leadership, discipline, and political morality. In the Indian context, a strong democratic tradition rooted in the society, secular character (in spite of communal politics); increasing awareness among the citizens (in the face of illiteracy and poverty); political sensitivity reflected in the voting behaviour; a strong (and independent) Fourth Estate and extensive network of non-governmental development organisations; and people's participation in the debate and development process constitute the base for democratisation.

The relative openness with which an Indian legislator approaches his tasks is in sharp contrast to the conservatism of the judiciary projected as judicial independence, and the insular disposition of the bureaucracy. This relative openness, as a strength of the legislators, is also revealed when viewed in the context of the "know-all" disposition of the administrators, and that of the judiciary that perceives its role as "supreme", and not so much as "complementary". Yet another relative strength of the legislative process in India is that all the political parties swear by the Constitution and 'constitutionalism' even when they differ on specific provisions, and issues.

The range of legislative support services, the inputs to enhance the effectiveness of legislators, fall into four distinct sets viz., imparting knowledge and skills, value-attunement, and cultural conditioning. These sets of inputs have to be related to the profile of legislators on the one hand, and their legislative roles on the other. Indeed, viewed from the long-term demands of democratisation and development, such support services should encompass "building up" of the various political cadres as a nursery to legislative career.

Under ideal democratic conditions, legislatures articulate the problems of the people, defining and prioritising them, harmonising the diverse and occasionally conflicting values, identities and interests underlying the issues. As all the elected representatives solemnly swear by the Constitution, legislative process should promote and reinforce consensualism over constitutional agenda. The legislatures are entrusted with the task of overseeing the administrative apparatus, ensuring transparency, and translation of legislated agenda into action. They are also assigned the task of facilitating, ensuring and monitoring the justice delivery system. What appears, in reality, to the naked eye of the public is at wide variance from what was envisioned and provided for in the Constitution.

An overview reveals that nation-building is not only neglected, but also distorted. The basic process of power, the electoral process is not yet stabilised in the Indian democracy. In such an unstable state, it can not promote a mission-mode of governance. A wide range of committees of legislature have been provided for by the Constitution itself with room for more innovations. The legislatures and legislative committees have been performing with varying degrees of efficacy, but certainly not to their full creative potential. The malignancy that has afflicted the political structures and electoral system is the primary factor that has negated the efficacy of legislative committees. The citizens are a mute witness to a perennial debate over reform, sans matching action. As they can not remain mute for all times, in a democracy, legislative inadequacies can contribute to social turbulence.

The duration of legislative sessions is progressively reduced almost to the statutory minima, due to political 'expediency'. 'But, the committees meet during the interregnum keeping members busy, and on the move, in order to make good the 'loss' of allowances to the members and thus as a safeguard to contain their potential for political mischief. Legislative behaviour is negotiated and compromised, *a la* 'match-fixing'. The legislative debates generate heat rather than light; often obstructionist and confrontationist, with increasing disorder, and criminal behaviour within the legislatures. The rock bottom of this scenario is that even the crimes under the penal law of the land are sought to be covered under immunities. Majorities are contrived as though numbers is all about democracy. Marshals take over within the legislatures with increasing frequency, and occasional additional support from civil police. 'Marshal law' within the legislatures is on the increase.

The only serious debate is on privileges, unrelated to protection and promotion of their functional efficacy. The only issue adopted without a debate, and silent consensualism is about salaries, allowances, pension and perks. Putting on the shield of privileges, people's representatives shun their status as citizens. Anti-defection law and party-whip are used, trampling upon freedom of expression and the responsibility to express without fear. This was demonstrated even in regard to the responsibility of the legislature as the only constitutional mechanism available to provide the much needed correctives to the judicial institutions, processes and faltering judicial functionaries.

Legislative policy, programme and strategy are found rarely consistent with the manifesto of the parties, the mandate given by the people and accountability to translate the democratic/electoral verdict. What is worse, dramatic measures are adopted, including amendments to the Constitution with a high political drama, but without a democratic mandate. The direct consequences of the pattern of behaviour of legislators and their collective legislative behaviour are that instead of legislatures discussing the problems of the people, the citizens are left with discussing the problems of legislatures, with the consequence of a growing disdain for political process itself. That the political functionaries themselves are disenchanted with their performance is reflected in their deflection of public concern into a debate over Parliamentary versus Presidential form of democracy. Citizens wonder whether such a debate is wrapped in any hidden agenda. The debate on Presidential versus Parliamentary form was started in 1950, remained live, though sporadic. All the time, and all the parties expressed the apprehension that the party in power, momentarily, would abuse constitutional changes to bring in an 'authoritarian' government. The pattern of debate reveals consistency over the projected motivation of the 'ruling' party. The ineffectiveness of parliamentary democracy in India, *per se*, is no vindication of the presidential form. That such a debate over the system could be an alibi for non-performance was apprehended by no less a person than Dr. Ambedkar, when he observed, in his concluding address to the Consembly that "if things go wrong – the reason will not be that we had a bad Constitution – man was vile".[15]

The Gandhian ethos, "my life is my message", philosophy of conviction and practice as a life-style have faded away. It was Gandhi, and his spiritual heir *Lok Nayak J.P.*, who reiterated that power is a trust, that all those who exercise power in society are accountable to the society, as trustees. Such an ethos cannot be mandated, but has to be nurtured and translated into reality by the leadership. The Quit India Resolution at the Indian National Congress (1942) categorically declared that "when power comes, it shall not belong to the Congress but to the entire people of India". It was in this context, advising the dissolution of the Indian National Congress, as the mainstream national party, Gandhi warned : "If instead of remaining the servants of the people, Congressmen become their masters. I may be alive or not, revolution will sweep over the country and the people will pick out the white-capped ones individually and finish them".[16]

In the Constituent Assembly and the provisional parliament there was no organised opposition. Only

22 members were in the category of 'unattached members' in 1950, it became 28 in 1951. But within the Congress itself there was a vocal section, which performed the role of an articulate opposition. Issues were debated openly and vigorously, both within the party and the parliament. The transformation of contemporary political organisations and culture in India can be seen as falling into three phases viz., (a) mobilisation for political freedom and social reform, (b) transformation of a movement into structures of power, and (c) setting in of malignancies in the political process. The abiding sustenance of the 'power' of political process was 'morality'. Power and morality represented two sides of the coin, the only currency of leadership. Humanist values constituted their ideology during the intense phase of the struggle for political freedom. Alleviation of poverty, elimination of illiteracy and disease, and promotion of social reform and justice constituted the mission of the leadership. Political freedom, economic growth with justice, and social development constituted an integral manifesto of the freedom movement.

The leadership of India's freedom movement comprised ardent nationalists, statesmen, reformists, and democrats with a profound respect for dissent, even as they strove for democratic consensus. They were charged by a missionary zeal. Their style was transparent, they transcended but never transgressed region, religion, caste or language. The leadership represented a case of 'sacrifice', like princes becoming paupers, they gave their all for the cause of national freedom and resurgence. They represented the qualities of a lion characterised by courage of conviction, and commitment to action. The dominant characteristics of contemporary leadership are equated with those of a fox, opportunist and cunning.

Power does not operate in a vacuum. As the British were preparing to leave, the omnibus Indian National

Congress quickly channeled into diverse streams; the post-independence scenario was marked by the emergence of a wide range of political parties, even as the INC remained an ombinus political chameleon. Like the Hindu pantheon, it became and remained an organisation providing for the co-existence of several, diverse, and conflicting ideological strands. If the INC proved the proverbial banyan tree during Nehru's times, it became strident under Indira Gandhi. The process of power blunted the constitutional ideals and the processes. Rajiv Gandhi attempted to bring about radical reform in the political as well as the administrative culture, but got devoured by the malignancy that had already set in. Narasimha Rao initiated a process of compulsive consensus, but where the political parties and processes were driven by 'personality-cult' leading to fragmentation, authoritarianism, arbitrary exercise of power without mandate, creation of vote-banks, and generation of discord between different sections of the people, the consensual process was fatally mowed down. Disintegration of political parties due to the exclusive pursuit of power had led to the inevitable consequence of fracturing the Indian polity, drowned in the consequential social strife.

As P.A. Sangma (one of the former Speakers of Lok Sabha) said, earlier there was one dominant party in power and several small parties, opposed to one another, in the opposition. Now the position has been reversed. We have a number of small parties opposed to each other, forming the government and one major party in the opposition. The small groups constantly formed a large variety of permutations with their 'stock value' fluctuating by the hour of the day, distorting in the process the democratic equilibrium. A great threat to democratic polity in India is that this political distortion is seen as a process of 'coalition politics', and all the parties are steadying for this pattern as a 'coalition era', of sharing power and exercising authority without accountability to either an agenda of action or norms of constitutional democracy.

The paradox emerges from the fact that the parties that emerged in almost all regions of the country, on the basis of local agenda, proclaimed that they were more 'nationalist' than the parties operating at the national level. They went one step further in accusing the national-level parties as being more regional. The fault-line emerges from the fact that some of them coalesced to become a federal front, but none have been able to play much of a positive role in resolving any of their bilateral or multilateral problems, or in cooperating with each other on matters of common concern. All political parties, national or regional, have raked-up popular emotions, and channelised them into hostilities, and violent conflicts among the people.

The enervation of political structures was accentuated by two related factors; the non-pursuit of Directive Principles, so as to promote socio-economic change as a part and process of nation-building; and the hasty incorporation of two ill-defined expressions viz., "secular" and "socialist" into the Preamble more as a strategy of partisan politics. The phenomenon of competitive populism has set in a process of ignoring the Directive Principles on the one hand, and incorporating the same as a new set of Fundamental Rights. Suffice it to say that incalculable damage has been caused to the letter as well as the spirit of the Constitution. The Preamble instead of sustaining the vision, and reinforcing the liberal democratic ethos, has itself been reduced as a malignant source in fracturing the Indian polity into majorities and minorities, a majority of minorities, and into the 'haves' and 'have-nots'. It could be seen as a confession that the political system could not ameliorate the conditions of the poorest of the poor. What is even worse, poverty and communal identities are being frozen, aggregated and converted into vote-banks.

Indian political organisations have acquired and internalised the corporate vocabulary such as 'Joint Ventures', mergers, take-overs, privatisation and capturing the markets (vote-banks, booths, legislative majorities) and sale (of tickets) – all that is part of 'corporate culture', with a dominant ethos of 'investments' and 'returns'. The style of public campaigns demonstrate that the political parties have surpassed corporate organisations.

Anti – defection law has not only failed in promoting democratic discipline in the political system, it has also led to the process of 'liberalised' politics in India. The splits and mergers of political groups and parties are accomplished with greater finess than the mergers and take-overs in the corporate sector, with single minded dedication to power and pelf. The short cuts to capturing power through the deployment of money-power, and lateral entry straight into the parliament are in tune with corporate culture, and in sharp contrast to the earlier mode of 'schooling for democracy' at Panchayat / Municipal levels and graduating to state assemblies and onwards to the national parliament.

If the 'princes' became paupers during the freedom movement, today's leadership represents a case of 'rags to riches' coupled with a vulgar display of ill-gotten wealth and the authoritarian exercise of power. The distortions of the political process have contributed to black money, parallel economy, and financial scams leading to the attraction of 'con-men', 'god-men' and criminal talent into politics.

The great debate of yester-years on the ends and means of social transformation is reduced to isolated crafting of manifestos, never related to action, much less to any measurement of performance. On the contrary, dramatic constitutional amendments and programmes such as nationalisation and reservations were initiated as a part of the game of power. Even as they have failed the Constitution and the nation, some of our political elite have initiated a campaign against the Constitution, stating that the "Constitution has failed the people". The consequences of the malignancy that has afflicted the political processes proved to be even more intense and dangerous to the process of democracy and governance, as is being witnessed and experienced in India. Wherever the political process turns malignant, it spreads rapidly and shows up, as the first symptom, in terms of degeneration and decay in the institutions of governance. Institutional decay has taken several forms such as 'nexus', and in terms of 'role-conflict' as is being witnessed as between the legislative and judicial institutions.

The political process cannot insulate itself from the social strife and institutional decay that it has created. The over-all apathy among the citizens towards the political process has contributed to the 'negative' vote or 'rejection' of the party in power, consistently in successive elections. Even worse, the price that all the political parties are paying at the hands of institutions like the Intelligence Bureau (IB) and the Central Bureau of Investigation (CBI), should remind our political elite of the Frankenstein, or its Indian version of the *Bhasmasura* phenomenon. The prime movers of constitutional democracy in India have changed over from being 'mission-driven' to 'power-driven'; the vision is lost sight of. When political party functionaries who are elected or appointed to positions of umpiring such as a Speaker or a Governor continue to be active members of their respective party for all intents and purposes, and later alternate in party-based positions as members of cabinet, the spirit of the Constitution gets vitiated.

Jawaharlal Nehru emphasised the challenge of political freedom and democracy, when he observed in the Constituent Assembly that "Freedom and power bring responsibility - - - - the future is one of incessant striving so that we might fulfil the pledges".[17] Dr. Ambedkar reminded us of the critical relevance of the quality of leadership inorder to work democracy and deliver its fruits to the people of India. Lok Nayak Jaya Prakash Narayan succinctly put : "In a parliamentary democracy, a citizen's life is governed in a large measure by the quality and content of the policy measures and laws adopted by parliament, state legislatures, municipal councils and panchayats. These in turn depend upon the quality and caliber of the elected representatives of the people". All the representatives who get elected cannot in fairness, be expected to have a prior adequate understanding of the type of competence needed for effectively participating in the debate on a variety of complex issues which come up for legislation and policy formulation. But, if proper facilities, appropriate to their status and requirements, are made available to them, it is reasonable that they would welcome it. Such facilities would be a boon not only to those who avail of them but could also result in better informed, more rational and mature, purposeful and responsive democratic institutions thereby strengthening the democratic fiber of the nation as a whole".[18]

The need for such ogranised inputs has acquired criticality due to some of the factors such as (a) initial impetus provided by the freedom movement as the fountainhead of value-orientation has faded away in less than three decades. (b) legislative activity has expanded and diversified into a complex task that transcends 'academic' inputs provided by the educational system, (c) local institutions of *Panchayat Raj* have ceased to be 'schools of democracy' due to the increasing degree of lateral entry into the state legislatures and the national parliament.

It is not that the politicians of today as a group do not have, among themselves, a large number of members from the diverse professions, like there were during the freedom movement. But, the fact is today's literate and professionals operate without the values and ethics that freedom fighters and the founding fathers had in abundance. Apart from the requisite range and level of knowledge and skills of analysis and monitoring that would enhance the capabilities of legislators, the legislators have to be impacted with the values and positive attitudes that would strengthen democratic ethic, constitutional conventions and political morality. Ethics Committees have been set up on several occasions but have yet to create any impact. The periodic Speakers' conferences have consistently resolved for the setting up of institutions designed to impart requisite skills and values, but the resolutions have not yet fructified into reality. The one positive aspect of elected representatives and political executives is their general perception of their inadequacies and an aptitude to acquire knowledge, skills and values of democratic governance, coupled with willingness to go through the learning process.

3.4. The Managers :

Administrative System :

Under the Westminster pattern of governance, there is considerable autonomy of the bureaucracy. There is a clear demarcation between the responsibilities of the political/elected functionaries and of the administrators appointed to the executive branch of government. The function of the political executive is to lay down policy, have that policy enacted into laws and the manner of its administration stipulated in the rules and regulations made under the enactments. The actual administration is undertaken by the duly empowered bureaucracy. Individual cases are not normally referred to the Minister unless it involves an exception to the policy laid down or has political repercussions. Thus, the bureaucracy provides a strong check on the arbitrary exercise of powers by the political executive. The political executive can alter policies, but cannot show undue favours to anybody. In India, however, almost from the very beginning, ministers have decided individual cases; this became the rule rather than the exception, especially so in the states. Consequently, the administration is rendered partisan, and ineffective. The exercise, misuse and abuse of powers of transfer, suspension, of promotion and postings of administrators are used by ministers to make the civil servants subservient to their will. In the Westminster pattern the power of appointments, transfers, promotions, suspensions and disciplinary action are all decided by a group of senior civil servants. These are of course subject to the approval of the Prime Minister (but no other minister). However, by convention that approval is normally not withheld.

As many as five Articles of the Constitution of India are devoted to protect the interests and autonomy of the bureaucracy, aimed at promoting neutrality, efficiency and effectiveness. Yet, the ground realties reveal that much of the bureaucracy has become pliable, adversely affecting not only its efficiency but also its image so much that one of India's Prime Ministers observed : "when the politicians expect the bureaucrats to bend, they crawl". Nowhere is this disposition more predominant, than in the case of law-enforcing organisations. Well formulated and articulated reform is anathema, inspite of continued abuse, misuse and non-use of police organisations, eroding their autonomy and accountability. This situation prompted one of the Presidents of India to plead, while in office openly, against the use of police in a partisan manner, for political ends.

The bureaucratic steel-frame, operated by the Indian Civil Service (ICS) performed its role of maintaining 'stability' commendably, even without any constitutional safeguards of service. Thereafter, the Indian Administrative (and other all India) Services took over with a role-shift from the maintenance of 'status quo' to socio-legal engineering aimed at the fulfilment of constitutional agenda. This role-shift warranted an orientation of 'service', social re-engineering, operating as the 'first court of Justice', while ensuring rule of law. The span of the role got expanded as to include a range of tasks such as promotion of awareness and empowerment of the public, implementation and monitoring of developmental programs, delivery of services, and providing feed-back to the political executive inorder to constantly fine-tune the policies. This expanded role has earned the appointed executive the labels of 'agents of change' and 'catalysts'. It has warranted, in the first place, honing of their skills of working with people, true to 'participative' democracy, and a reorientation of their work ethic (values, attitudes and performance standards) in tune with the demands of democratisation, and participative development.

The role-shift and expanded role in the context and ambience of democratisation and development warranted a transformation from within, as an essential prerequisite to be able to perform the role and modus assigned by the Constitution. Democratisation and participative development warranted, *inter alia*, (a) openness, in place of secretiveness and abuse of 'information as power', (b) citizen participation in place of dependence and alienation leading to a 'distance' between the two, (c) decentralisation in place of centralisation and hierarchical barriers, (d) political neutrality, (e) result-orientation instead of conformity to rules *per se*, (f) mission orientation i.e. dedication to public service in place of 'careerism' (g) conviction and commitment to democratic ethic, characterised by integrity, honesty, trust and empowerment of the citizens so as to promote self reliance and a movement towards more governance with less and less of government. The reality is that in five decades, administration has not changed to any significant degree, instead it stands out as the major stumbling block to democratisation and development. The explicit constitutional provision (73rd and 74th Amendments) of decentralisation have not fructified due to the frozen state of bureaucratic 'centralisation', hierarchical and authoritarian disposition. This disposition is widely reflected in the content and methods of 'orientation' progammes designed and developed by the administrators for the elected representatives of the *Panchayati Raj* Institutions (PRIs) and municipal corporations. The emphasis continues to be on 'tailoring' the performance of elected representatives to the bureaucratic rules and procedures. The administrators continue to impede the agenda and cripple the style of elected representatives.

Inorder to ensure that the best brains give of their best performance, there is an extensive motivational package of (a) multiplication of levels inorder to provide promotional opportunities (b) time-bound schemes of pay increases and promotions (c) compensation for increases in cost of living (six national-level Pay Commissions in five decades) (d) perquisites relating to housing, transport, medical, holiday homes and travel packages (e) terminal benefits, and (f) welfare and social security measures such as life-time as well as family pension, chain of cooperative stores with priority supplies at fair-prices. If the Constitution provides for measures, spanning five Articles, protecting conditions of service especially to the all India services, the other levels are protected even more by the trade-unions rights. These extensive safeguards are not available to the citizens of the nation. In fact all these benefits are provided at the expense of the citizens, in the hope of efficient and effective performance on the part of the administrative functionaries. That the administrators do not perceive themselves as citizens in the first place was dramatically revealed by the spontaneous observations of the 'Head' of a Department, at a farewell function thus : "From tomorrow onwards, I have to learn to live as an ordinary citizen". It is frightening for the administrators even to imagine life as an ordinary citizen, without the power and privileges that go with an office.

Government servants push the files for not more than 150 days per year, (the rest are all holidays); administration takes more than 85 paise out of every Rupee revenue, the community gets less and less out of the balance of 15 paise, as the administrative structures proliferate, and, increasing cost of living is neutralised, while the common man is exposed to the cost of living spiral.

India has to infuse the democratic ethos into the administration, which continues to operate with a colonial mindset. In the Indian Republic, 'public servants' do not seem to consider themselves as citizens of the Republic; they are not accessible to the 'average citizens; they look down upon the citizens as lesser mortals.

All the ombudsmen institutions ranging from anticorruption bureaux; grievance and complaint mechanisms; vigilance cells and commissioners; *Lok Ayuktas* and the much debated *Lok Pal*; and a wide range of other national and state level commissions (women, human rights, minorities, etc.) have not been able to mitigate, much less eradicate the problems of citizens with the administration. These ombudsmen institutions represent a pyramid of pyramids as depicted in Illustration 3.6, daunting the citizens of India. This pyramid of pyramids appears to be built in advance, as the final resting place of democracy in India.

The 'average' citizen's disposition towards the political / legislative as well as the administrative institutions and processes is characterised by fear, frustration, indignation, antagonism, and hostility. Ordinary citizens are alienated and turned into rebels, because of collusion between the political and the administrative functionaries.

Recognising that democratic social transformation and good governance necessitate, in the first place, restructuring of the institutions and processes of governance and a change in the mind-set of the executive functionaries, a series of reform exercises were initiated. The chronicle of exercises involved considerable costs of time and finances, and aroused the expectations of the people whose hopes appeared to be proverbially eternal. The changes in the administration so far have been confined to tinkering of the structures, proliferation of institutions and tiers leading to sky-rocketing administrative costs, and, the citizens being shunted from 'pillar to post'. The so called, 'single-window' approach, promised *ad nauseam*) has resulted only in additional windows. Resistance to change and vested interests emerge as the prime factors that have stalled reform. This resistance to change has negated some innovative

ILLUSTRATION 3.6

ILLUSTRATIVE PYRAMID OF PYRAMIDS

Indian Pantheon for Managing Institutional Malfunctioning

STATUS

LEVEL

AUTONOMOUS LEGISLATIVE JUDICIAL EXECUTIVE CIVIL SOCIETY

STATUTORY CONSTL. QUASI QUASI

INTNTL

UN WTO Sec. Coun. Transparency International

NATIONAL

BAR COUNCIL
MEDICAL COUNCIL
MEDIA COUNCIL
ASCI
UGC
UNIVERSITIES

PARLIAMENT
HOUSE COMMITTEE
CH. VIG. COMM.
C & AG
SPEAKER
ETHICS COMMITTEE
RBI

PRESIDENT
SUPREME COURT
LOK PAL
CH. EL ECTION COMMI SSION
JUDICIAL COMMISSION
DEPTL. COMM.
NATNL. COMMISSION
HU.RIGHTS MINORITY SCEST
WOMEN, CHILDREN
REGULATORY INSTNS.

P.M.
PMO
CABINET
PRASAR BHARATI/ CBI IT
TRAI/IRDC/ERA DIRECTORATE
DEPT. OF PERSONNEL
DEPTS. – UNITS 3 TIER MECH.

SOC. ADT.

STATE

UNIVERSITIES
CHARTERED AUDITORS
VIGILANCE PSUs/DEPTT.

LEGISLATURE
HOUSE COMMITTEE
VIG. COM.
A & A.G.
SPEAKER

GOVERNOR
HIGH COURT
LOK AYUKTA
ADMN. TRIBUNALS
JUDICIAL/ COMMISSIONS/ DEPT. COMMS.

CM
CMO
CABINET
Anti Com. Bureau
DEPTL. UNITS 3-TIER TECH.
COMPLAINTS GRIEVANCES

CIVIL LIBERTIES
HUMAN RIGHTS VIGIL ORGZNS
Social Audit
Consumer Grounds
GOONDAS
EXTREMISTS

LOCAL

MEDIA COLUMNS
EMPOWERMENT CAMPAIGNS

PRIs
DARBARS

DIST. JUDICIARY
REGISTRAR OF COOPS.
CONS UMER COU RTS
LOWER COURTS
POL ICE
DARBARS

CASTE PANCHAYATS
NGOs
CBOs

CITIZENS IN SEARCH OF PATHS OF SALVATION

political initiatives such as citizens charters, social audit, and technology missions. Any debate on reform continues to lead towards the stock adage "*man versus system*". We have tinkered with the structures but have not been able to change the mind-sets, which appear to be frozen. Mecaulay believed the non-European religions and cultures as nothing more than paganism. It was this value-disposition that prompted him to ask the British civil servants to treat Indians as an inferior race. This has led to a progressive demoralisation of the Indian psyche. The post-Independence administrative ethos has further degenerated into pushing citizens into servility.

There is considerable dissonance and continuing debate on the role relationships between ministers and civil servants. They have not yet settled, but what is universally recognised in India is that there is considerable mutual negation in the role-relationships between these two categories of functionaries. Sharing of the vision of India and willingness to work together on a mission mode constitute the essential prerequisites for promoting complementary and synergic relationship. An overview of the patterns of mutual relationships between the political executives and administrators reveals four-fold dispositions as indicated in Illustration 3.7. Each of these four patterns has a different impact on the quality of governance. First pattern is characterised by a shared vision, complementarity and creative interaction, leading to reinforcement of the system, peak performance, and a high level of public esteem. The second one shows that the vision is blurred, a sense of withdrawal becomes evident, with a fear of decision-making, leading to low-voltage performance, and loss of credibility, with the consequence of low public esteem. The third pattern reveals a loss of vision, adversary relations, and mutual negation with the

ILLUSTRATION 3.7
CONSTITUTIONAL VISION
MISSION MODE OF GOVERNANCE OFFICIAL NON-OFFICIAL INTERFACE

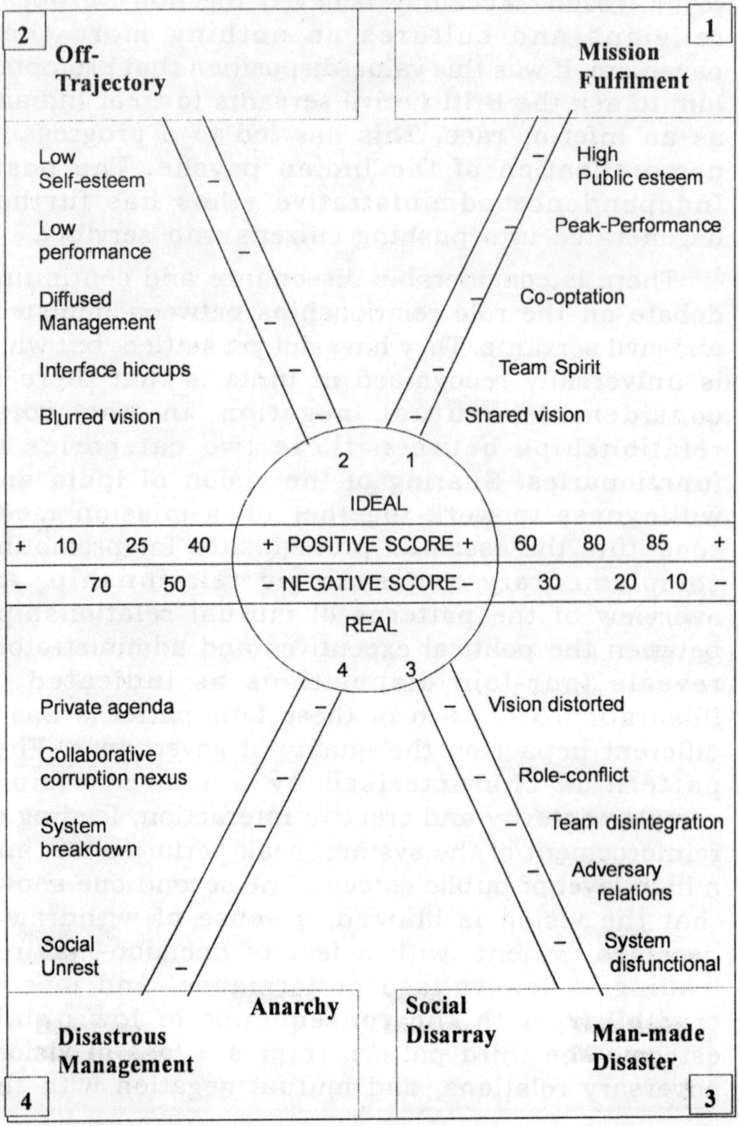

consequence of a dysfunctional system, low performance, and social disarray. The fourth one reveals pursuit of partisan / private agenda, collusion and collaborative exploitation with the consequences of administrative breakdown, public hostility and social turbulence. Whatever may be the specific pattern of relationship in specific situations, there has emerged an unholy alliance between the political executives and the administrators. This is demonstrated by innumerable instances that emerged into a constant pattern of administrators appointed to "oversee" the development works undertaken by the Panchayati Raj and other peoples organisations. However, it may be safely stated that in India as a whole, the dispositions have not been uniform but varying; they are fluctuating, but characterised by a steady, continuing downward slide.

Every incoming political party forming the government, at the national as well as those in the states, starts off with a massive bureaucratic "shake-up". Witch-hunting has taken such deep roots that just for the honest expression of an opinion, an officer constantly fears and frequently faces summary transfer, if he is lucky; and CBI raids, cooked-up charges, suspension and departmental proceedings if he is not so lucky. Politicians behave in a manner diametrically opposite to what Sardar Patel enjoined them to do, yet garland the Sardar's statue, every year, ritualistically.

It is these non-performing patterns and the pursuit of private agenda that drive the citizens towards corrupt practices, or drive them away from the administration, the first court of justice, to the second court with the hope of securing justice, either through Public Interest Litigation (PIL) or through the regular, hierarchical track of the judicial system. More and more, though not all, hapless victims of non-performing or malfunctioning administration undertake their 'pilgrimage of hope' to the court system. The Supreme Court cautioned the administration by saying : "don't leave the governance to the Court". The bench (comprising justice B.N. Kirpal and Justice K.G. Balakrishna) directed the Center to "indicate as to how it will ensure that the schemes formulated by it are implemented so that benefit is received by those for whom they are intended".[19] The civil services and the 'bureaucratic politics' have to take the blame as much as the partisan politicians. Fixing administrative accountability, a three judge bench of the Supreme Court (headed by the then Chief Justice B N Kirpal) fixed the responsibility for the continuing starvation deaths on the Chief Secretaries of states on the basis of a report prepared by the Court Commissioners on the implementation of various poverty alleviation programmes. Inspite of an extensive network of administrative tribunals, the Supreme Court had to step in, with increasing frequency, to provide correctives to the administrative process. This is illustrated by the directions such as (a) the Supreme Court directs the CBI to file FIRs against a Chief Minister, (b) the Court directs the government to formulate norms providing for fixed tenures to the IPS officers, and (c) the Supreme Court frowns on the government of India on the appointment of a bureaucrat as Competition Commissioner. During the times of competitive populism between the politicians and bureaucrats, it is refreshingly pleasant to note a senior IAS officer refusing an award as an "outstanding bureaucrat" on grounds that "public awards, felicitations and honours were for public personalities and not for bureaucrats".

Dilution of the standards and levels of 'neutrality' and service orientation on the one hand, and expansion and diversification of corrupt practice within the bureaucracy on the other have increased the volume of Public Interest Litigation (PIL), and repeated strictures by the judiciary on the partisan conduct of administrators. The reluctance and failure to uphold rule of law on the part of the executive has led to a breakdown, in the aggregate, of the system of constitutional democracy. The emergence of PIL has renewed the hope of the common man. But the Judicial system was not equipped to meet the surge of PIL.

Judicial System

A critical strength of the judicial system in India has been the high level of awareness on the part of its leadership of the urgent need to enhance the efficacy and effectiveness of the system, and to overcome the negative image caused and contributed to by historical factors such as inaccessibility, delays due to procedural and human factors, and discriminatory as well as unaffordable costs.

The consistent pile-up of pending litigation at various levels of the judiciary is discussed *ad nauseum,* both by the legislatures and the judicial leadership. But the volume of dockets is growing faster than the frequency of debates. In fact, these 'debates' have not taken cognizance that there are a lot more citizens who prefer not to take their problems to the court system because of the perceived loss of credibility of the system. If statistics of this category are also computed, the volume of clogged litigation would constitute an indictment of the judicial system itself.

When the political / legislative process is distorted due to competitive populism, and focussed on the pursuit of power at an enormous social cost, and as the administrative process has become self-serving, the damned social problems explore and pursue alternative tracks, in search of solutions. That is how, in India today, the judicial system has moved to the centre-stage of public debate while social problems moved on to the path of people taking law into their hands. Lawlessness, social strife and myriad manifestations of extremism, threaten to drown the state as well as the process of rule of law.

Under conditions of a democratic decentralised polity, the ideal of '*Rama Rajya*' should have been 'empty-court-rooms', and 'zero-litigation' – between citizens as well as between citizens and the state. But in reality, we are carrying on with an antiquated legal system and Judicial process even after 50 years of Independence. The system frustrates the law-abiding citizens most; the conscientious members of the Judiciary are equally frustrated with the realisation that they are manning a system that has become dysfunctional, counter-productive and immersed in diverse mutations of corruption. All this in spite of the volumes of reports being churned out by the national and state level law commissions, and various other reform commissions and committees that invariably end up, *inter-alia,* with a beaten path of recommendations such as (a) amendments to the existing provisions of law (b) improvements in the content and quality of legal education, and (c) increasing the number of judges at various levels *et al.* An adjunct to this set is the reform of the Judicial structures, processes, training and continuing education for members of the Judiciary at all levels. The most note-worthy is the fact that India has excelled itself in the proliferation of institutions but certainly not in initiating reform, in promoting a 'work-ethic', and a mission mode of functioning.

There is a tremendous amount of filtration (complaints are not registered, often the aggrieved party is slighted, insulted and even abused in a variety of ways beyond the verbal, in police stations).

There occur debilitating process distortions at the chambers of advocates as well as in the court premises. It has become proverbial, that the 'rich', 'influential' and 'knowledgeable' threaten the poor, the weak, the innocent and the ignorant, that they will be 'dragged to the court'. The innocent, who have no other means of pursuing redressal of their problems, are aware that it is the rich, the influential and the underworld who are abusing; and are allowed by the system to abuse the judicial process. In fact the Judicial system in India today has to save itself from drowning, before it can save the aggrieved citizens and thus save the Rule of Law, the foundational premise of our constitutional democracy. There was a Judge who while dealing with alienation of tribal land, spontaneously even if unwittingly stated "but what would happen to the "poor" people who invested a lot of money on the lands?" There is a need for attunement between the values of the Constitution and that of its umpires viz., the members of the Judiciary.

Even more dangerous to the Republic is the image, that is gaining ground, of systemic inadequacies and distortions in the appointments, transfers and elevations of members of the Judiciary, and increasing degrees and myriad forms of corruption creeping into the managerial processes of the Judicial system. True to the extant culture of governance in India, 'transfer' as an effective instrument of 'punishment' is being used, though fluctuating from time to time, even in the case of Judiciary. What is worse, post retirement appointments have emerged as incentives and 'rewards' for 'creditable' performance. Providing legislative cover to such appointments transgressing the spirit of the Constitution represents yet another form of degeneration, contributing to the loss of credibility of the political as well as judicial sub-systems, the two critical sub-systems of governance. There is an oft repeated argument for maintaining the ratio between the number of judges and the growing population. The judicial leadership must give up this 'growth trajectory' and move in the direction of a wide range of innovative reforms, preventive and litigative strategies, higher levels of productivity including an increase in its working days from the existing average of less than 200 days per annum, and radical shift in the work ethic of Indian 'holidays' and court vacations. Most important of all, community based non-litigative dispute settlement and conflict resolution institutions and processes have to be innovated institutionalised, and promoted. The judicial leadership is a party to the creation of a wide range of esoteric tribunals, commissions and alternate dispute settlement mechanisms at the national and state levels; but it had not shown equal interest in creating and strengthening community level institutions such as *Nyaya Panchayats*. The frequency of 'inspection' from within the hierarchy is increasing no doubt, but with increasing distortions and diminishing returns. Judicial institutions reveal a high degree of hierarchy and unending layers of litigation. Citizens are at a loss to appreciate the rationale of judicial independence, and contempt jurisdiction. The judicial system has the unique advantage of the National Law Commission operating as a permanent 'in-house' resource. A number of reform measures aimed at making the judiciary deliver the constitutional promise are crying for attention and action.

The menace of 'approachability', corruption, and acts of moral turpitude are emerging to the fore with increasing frequency. There is a rapid slide in judicial accountability that has alienated the people and eroded the constitutional promise of the rule of law. These could deal a fatal blow to constitutional democracy in India, for no institution under the Constitution of India could escape the social audit by the people, the citizens.

The Constitution of India – voluminous and thus seemingly complex – is built on the strength of a complement of institutions. The units of this network have been assigned complementary 'tasks' to be performed in unison inorder to be able to fulfill the vision of the Constitution. The Constitution has assigned the roles to be performed together; without any *inter se* hierarchy. The roles and tasks assigned to the various functionaries and institutions cannot be juxtaposed in any adversarial, much less confrontationist framework of one versus the other.

All the instrumentalities of state – legislative, executive and judicial have, over a period of time, got derailed from the track of mission mode of governance. This derailment has been a consequence of deficiencies in the management of (a) internal efficacy in the respective institutions, (b) role conflict emerging from deficiencies in inter-face management (c) inadequacies in the performance by the wide-range of regulatory institutions (inspite of constitutionally defined roles and constitutional status), (d) inadequate citizens' social audit mechanisms, and vigilance institutions of civil society, (e) non-crystallisation and debasement of constitutional conventions and democratic traditions, and (f) impaired umpiring of the game of constitutional democracy.

The virus that afflicted the political and legislative processes could not be checked and contained by the Speakers of the legislatures, or the much publicised codes of conduct and ethics committees. The legislative effort to contain the virus that enervated the political system by the creation of an Election Commission suffered a distortion *ab initio*, as its status, role, design, manning norms were ill-defined. The subsequent enactment intended to remedy some of the distortions by making it a three-member body proved to be worse than the earlier design deficiency. The virus that afflicted the political environment not only defied a remedy but got virulent over time leading to partisan labelling of the Commissioners.

A chain of administrative tribunals was set up to promote and protect the interests of the administrative personnel, but none that would enforce their accountable performance of the assigned role. Some regulatory mechanisms intended to promote neutrality, transparency and accountability – such as the State Security Commissions – have not seen the light of the day. This collective indifference on the part of the legislatures towards ensuring administrative transparency and accountability, was inspite of all the political parties, in all the states as well as in the centre, consistently accusing the 'ruling' parties all over, of abusing and misusing the police for partisan ends. The police leadership has not raised their voice either in protest or in demanding autonomy, as if confirming the 'nexus' factor. The impression given is that, over a period of time, the comfort of operating under political patronage outweighs the value of professional autonomy, and accountability for performance. It is like a tiger accustomed to enjoying the comforts of a cage, that fears freedom. When the political virus has grown strong and spread wide in the Indian democracy, how can the Judicial limb keep itself above the rest and develop immunities? The inevitable consequence is a dilution in its role as the sustainer and protector of rule of law. The backlog of outdated legislative framework, structures, and system, and value dispositions which are in crying need of reform have added to the loss of credibility of constitutional democracy, in the aggregate.

As all the institutions of state have diluted their functional efficiency and effective management of their mission, their *inter-se* relations in terms of complementarity of tasks and common objectives suffered multiple afflictions. Even a brief over-view of governance process reveals the malignancy that warrants a 'multi-specialty' surgical intervention. Some of these malignancies are reflected in the form of (a) the draft bill on electoral reforms which defies disclosure norms set by the Supreme Court for would-be-legislators, (b) the focus, priorities and the modus of functioning of the National Human Rights Commission which kept on shifting with every new incumbent Chairperson in a manner as to warrant the Supreme Court, to stay the proceedings of NHRC; (c) three former Chief Justices moved the Gujarat High Court seeking to join as parties in a petition filed by an NGO against the NHRC; (d) a High Court issuing a restraint order on the Director General of Police who had been directed by the State Legislature (acting as a court) to produce a citizen accused of transgressing the privileges of the House; (e) two national level Commissions viz. the NHRC and the National Commission for Minorities (NCM) taking parallel decisions issuing different directions to a State Government, and (f) Patna High Court's orders barring undertrials from contesting elections.

The interface management of the legislative, executive and Judicial institutions has been cast by the Constitution in tune with the norms of liberal democracy, with the judiciary as the citadel of freedom and justice. The founding fathers, anxious to safeguard the independence of judiciary, provided for its freedom from partisan political influences. The court is not conceived as the third chamber. Thus the Constitution struck a delicate balance between parliamentary sovereignty and judicial supremacy. Towards this end, they have incorporated special provisions for upholding the independence of the Judiciary. It was in this spirit judges of the Supreme Court and of High Courts were debarred from appointment to offices of profit after retirement. Yet the legislation setting up the National Human Rights Commission defies the letter and spirit of the Constitution by stipulating the requirement of retired Chief Justices for appointment as Chairperson of the NHRC. Such provisions stand out as a potential agenda of public interest litigation.

The interface management has been distorted in practice in various ways leading to leakage as well as pilferage of power; cross-connections, short-circuits, and flash points. The situation may lead to a collapse of the power grid. Complementarity has turned into role-conflict and confrontationist dispositions seeking to establish *inter-se* supremacy on the one hand, and such *inter-se* management issues adversely affecting the levels of productivity of all the institutions. An overview of the organisational and *inter-face* management problems reveals that these problems do not emerge from any design deficiencies in the Constitution. They are not so much 'systemic' but almost entirely caused by human factors such as individual motivations of different actors and the collective organisational culture which are at variance with the constitutional values. These deficiencies and distortions are converted into a grand debate cast in the form of individuals versus systems/institutions.

It is in this perspective that the role efficacy of the protector and defender of the Constitution, the President of India assumes critical significance. Suffice to say at this point, that even the office of President as the constitutional ombudsman has been subjected to partisan pressures and prejudices. The constitutional spirit has been nullified by the manner of unseemly political discourse and the coloured "interpretation" of the 'letter' of the Constitution. 'Minority' labels, lack of 'political experience', and lack of exposure to constitutional law have been affixed to personalities not withstanding that the citizens consider that these and similar 'labels' do not represent the relevant attributes for the august office of the President of India.

Mission mode of governance cannot be initiated or promoted much less sustained by political resolutions, legislated norms, administrative circulars or Judicial pronouncements. Mission mode can be promoted by cultivating adequate and appropriate value 'dispositions' and attitudinal conditioning, sustained through conscious renewal. Mission mode calls for creative and committed leadership. Creating a positive and productive work ethic is a function of the quality of leadership in all organisations – be it a family, a business organisation or institutions of governance. It cannot be preached, but promoted by 'practice' as Mahatma Gandhi practiced, and reflected once, "*my life is my message*". Service orientation, acquisition and upgradation of requisite knowledge and skills, commitment to the norms of ethics, and social accountability are some of the qualities of leadership that contribute towards shaping organisational discipline, performance and synergy.

Managing the constitutional vision of India calls for leadership, equally of the legislative, judicial and executive institutions with conviction of and commitment to that vision. It is only when all the three streams of institutions share that vision it could be pursued and fulfilled, they can move together on the trajectory of constitutional roles and goals as projected in Illustration 3.8. Available evidence suggests that, over the span of five decades, the legislative and the executive institutions had deviated from the constitutional track, whereby we could not move in the direction of the constitutional goals. The judicial institutions had tried to operate as the 'countervailing force' and succeeded to a considerable extent, in correcting the deviance on the part of legislative and executive institutions and processes. But, with the gradual loss of equilibrium as between the legislative and the executive institutions, the judicial institutions not only failed in maintaining that equilibrium but contacted the malignancy, *a la* the doctor while trying to remedy the disease himself got afflicted.

ILLUSTRATION 3.8
TRAJECTORY OF CONSTITUTIONAL ROLES AND GOALS

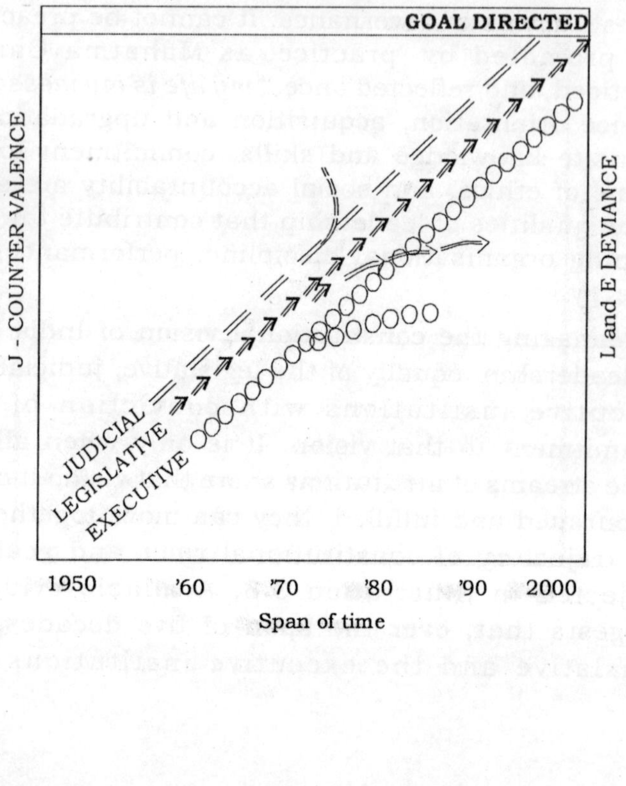

The situation obtaining today reminds us of what Nehru and Radhakrishna had stated in the Constituent Assembly. They were prophetic. Nehru observed "The service of India means the service of the millions who suffer . . . ." Dr. Radhakrishna was characteristic in his observations "our opportunities are great but let me warn you that when power outstrips ability, we will fall on evil days. . . . . . . "[20]

The increasing crescendo of debate on the need for a code of conduct for the legislators, administrators, judicial functionaries, law and order authorities and professionals such as doctors, lawyers, educationists, business and industry managers, and journalists reflects the reality of all-round deterioration in the ethical standards. Unless we take early corrective action in restoring political morality and ethical standards among all the institutions of the Republic, it will not be the mission-mode of governance that is at stake, but the democratic order itself. The leadership from all walks of the Indian society need to remind itself that decades ago we had ignited a global democratic movement, and about five decades ago envisioned to set standards of democratic governance as a role-model. Mission-mode of governance is not an esoteric rhetoric, but a vital prerequisite for democratic social transformation. We had emerged as the 'largest' democracy, and got stuck with that cliché, and self-deceit. We have to set ourselves to move on the path of democratic development inorder to achieve the status of a great democracy. That is the vision of our Constitution, it can be achieved only through a mission-mode of governance.

3.5. We the people

Gurajada, a great social thinker once observed that it is the people but not a territory that makes a nation. During the first five decades of freedom, India's population has grown nearly 233 per cent. The rate of population growth *per se* is projected as the single largest stumbling block of development. Population growth has remained a subject of intense and coloured political debate. This colouration has led to multiple fractures and fragmentation of the polity. The Indian society has failed itself in not evolving as a nation, with a sense of nationalism.

From the state of being the 'largest' democracy if India has to advance towards becoming a 'great' democracy, the only path available is for the 'demos' to assert and restore their citizenship. Citizenship and nationalism reflect the two positive attributes and constitute the foundations for democracy and participative development. Thus, citizenship, pride of citizenship to be precise, has to be seen as a qualitative characteristic of a community, not as a declaratory status. Decentralisation of governance and citizen participation have to be geared to integrate democracy and development in a mutually reinforcing relationship. The pluralist society has to be placed on the trajectory of self-reliant, sustainable and holistic development. Citizenship and nationalism have suffered grievously; a nation is alienated against itself and is in a 'state of disarray'. Anarchic conditions can not be labelled as problems of 'internal security', for such an explanation leads to a further slide into the state trampling upon human rights, and state-sponsored violence which is the very anti-thesis of the core liberal values of democracy. Violence and democracy do not mix; cannot co-exist for long. India has attained a state of Gross Social Conflict (GSC), disrupting development and threatening its democratic character. To add to this social disarray, the municipal, the state and the national level institutions of governance in India are locked-up with the citizens as adversaries reflected in terms of the growing volume of citizen-state litigation.

There are two attributes of democracy that operate as its inherent strengths. First, it has a capacity to sustain itself; i.e. democracy as a way of life is strengthened by the modes of democracy; second, in the ultimate analysis, when democracy is bottled up for too long, it breaks free. In the first characteristic both the ends and means are reinforced, in the second one the ends are reinforced, at the transient cost of the means. When democracy asserts itself, the demos gain, the leadership (including the elite group) suffer, grievously. Mission mode of governance focusses on appropriate methods, the means. If the means turn malignant, the demos reveal signs of demoralisation and demonstrate social rejection of the political malignancy manifest in terms of social turbulence, snowballing into a search for alternative paths, as indicated in Illustration 3.9. The leadership has to enhance its role efficacy and credibility not only in the interest of sustainable democracy but also in its own enlightened self-interest.

ILLUSTRATION 3.9

MISSION MODE OF MANAGEMENT

Managerial Dispositions and Paths of Development

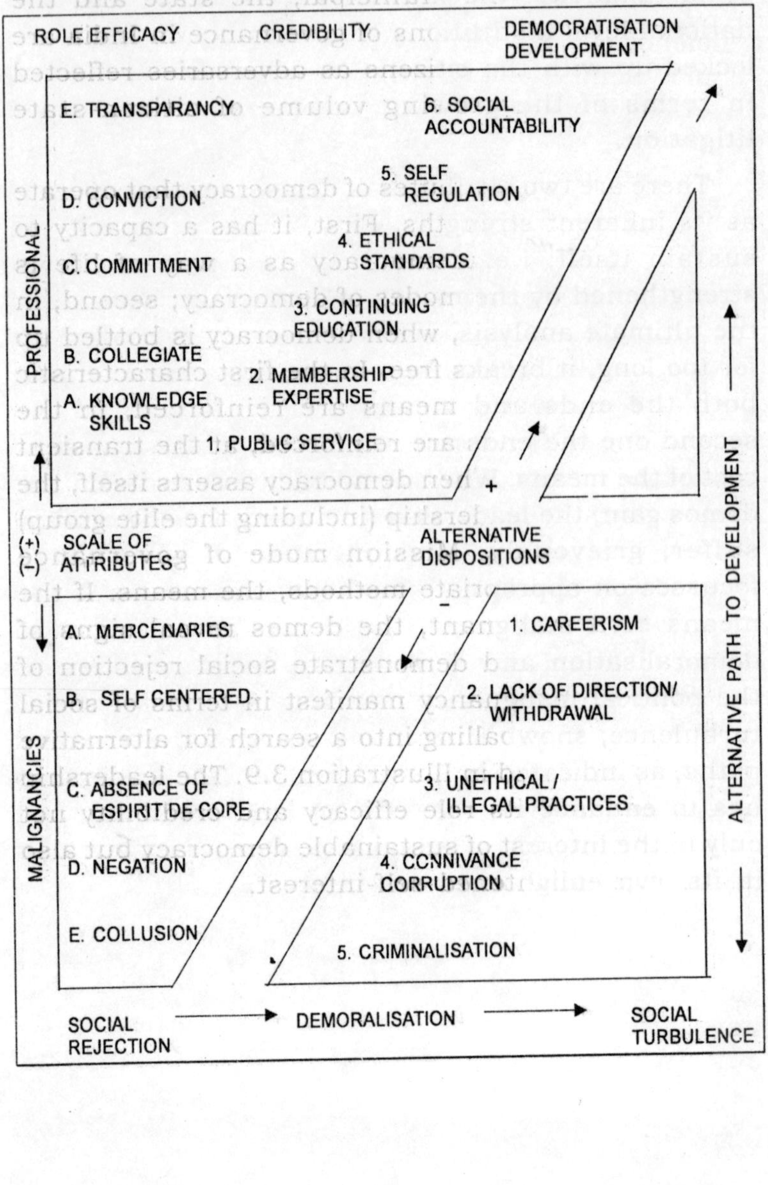

At the end of six Five Year Plans, the National Planning Commission had made a seminal observation that though considerable development has been registered, India's record of development did not match its potential and that much of the deficiency can be traced to lack of involvement of the people. Simultaneously the approach paper to the Seventh Plan (1984) forcefully brought out that planning and development had not utilised the potential of science and technology. In this background, it was resolved to promote, set up and strengthen *Panchayati Raj* Institutions (PRIs) as a strategy for decentralisation of structures and participation of people as a *sine qua non* for accelerated and sustainable development. Thus, the 1980s recognised the need to bring forth two hitherto untapped vital inputs viz., peoples' participation, and utilisation of science and technology inorder to accelerate the process of development in areas such as literacy, immunisation and drinking water. Participation and decentralisation operating as the two vital facets of democracy are critical to the promotion of responsible, responsive, accountable and transparent qualities of good governance.

The mass movement for political freedom was hinged on the participative process. However, soon after Independence, the national discourse on participative process in the democratic governance and social transformation was reduced to the structural relations of decentralisation as between the union and the sates, which got degenerated into a situation of confrontation and conflict. Decentralisation became an exercise in 'sharing of power' between the two-tiers. Political parties became power-centers with a highly centralised, authoritarian leadership, and thus ceased to be democratic even within their respective political parties. The authoritarian political leadership used and abused the administrative machinery in sustaining itself. The administrative leadership with its classical bureaucratic, hierarchical, authoritarian traits became a willing partner in the centralisation of power. People are excluded from the structures and processes of democracy, and got alienated from the political as well as bureaucratic processes in the 'largest' democracy. This explains the consistent anti-incumbency vote in India's democratic process – a process of alienation and rejection.

The 73rd and 74th amendments to the Constitution which accorded constitutional status to the *Panchayati Raj* Institutions of self-governance proved futile in the face of unresolved equations between the union and the states at one level, and the authoritarian political parties and the centralised bureaucracy at another level. The exercise in decentralisation ended up with a higher degree of 're-centralisation', in myriad ways. Citizens' participation has been, perhaps, the most distorted dimension of democracy in India. Alienation of citizens not only stalls, but distorts and negates the process of democracy. The concept and process of participation was not allowed to take roots, much less flourish, in all the spheres of democracy. India has yet to secure liberation from the bureaucratic legacy of the British, the steel-frame.

Liberal democracy represents an institutional process which makes it impossible for a few to abuse the power vested in them. It ensures that government remains continuously accountable to the citizens. Citizen participation ensures that (a) the elected representatives remain accessible all the time, (b) their problems will be resolved and that (c) common issues would promote integration and collective action where necessary.

A large number of innovations such as Citizens' Manifesto, Citizens' Charters, Social Audit have to be brought into vogue to facilitate citizens' participation and to ensure accountability and transparency of the political and administrative institutions.

The indifference of large sections of the so-called literate and affluent sections of the society. is as much responsible for the highjacking of the democratic process by political parties. It is this non-participative, non-assertive public that has encouraged political parties to dump all the vital reform measures recommended by more than 20 national level commissions and committees, and reduce the agenda of political and electoral reform into a single issue of public-funding of elections.

Special provisions for the administration of people in the Schedule Areas and members of Scheduled Tribes have been carved out by the Consembly in Schedules V and VI of the Constitution. In the case of the Scheduled Tribes and Tribal Areas (in states other than Assam) Tribes Advisory Councils (TACs) have been provided for inorder to enable members of the tribal communities to influence and shape the policies, and to guide the administration, in the promotion of their welfare. In reality, the TACs, constitutionally designed to protect the interests and to promote the welfare of tribal communities, have been sucked by the distortions of the mainstream political process.[21]

The proclaimed objectives and modes of self-governance and participative development should have, logically, seen a reduction in the role and hence the sise of 'governments' both at the union and state levels. But in reality, viewed from many an angle, there has been a phenomenal growth and proliferation in the structures, tiers, levels and numbers of 'public servants' both at the centre and state levels. Instead of a redefinition of the role of government and governance as a part of the process of decentralised democracy, and a possible reduction in size, the contrary has been witnessed. Citizens ended up with an excess of government, excesses of state, and diminishing governance. A number of regulatory mechanisms that have been set up, in the sphere of public utilities became almost adjunct units of government, with the adoption of same features of structures, rules and the bureaucratic mind-sets.

Very soon in the nascence of our Republic, the trinity of institutions – legislative, executive and judicial, have edged the people out, and never allowed a feeling that they too had a participatory role in the working of the Constitution. Instead of the political parties, the prime movers and the legislatures discussing the problems of the people, the citizens are left discussing the problems generated by the political parties and the legislatures in particular, and the process of governance in general. An assertive and articulate public opinion has demonstrated the vibrancy of democracy in India as witnessed at least on three occasions – first when the 'emergency' had been nipped in the bud by the people; second, when legislation seeking to censor the media had to be withdrawn; and third, when the efforts to curb public interest litigation were made futile. Politicians and political parties are not alone. The other elites, the intellectuals, the professions, leadership of business and industry have equally contributed to the degeneration establishing that political degeneration cannot be contained within the political structures. All the elite groups today reflect the seven sins that Mahatma Gandhi abhorred:

Politics without principles

Wealth without work

Pleasure without conscience
Knowledge without character
Commerce without morals
Science without humanism
Worship without sacrifice

During the colonial period, equations between the 'rulers' and the 'subjects' were such that violation of rules, regulations, or law by the subjects was labelled as 'criminal' / 'indiscipline' whereas such violation on the part of rulers would merely give rise to 'grievances' of the people. It was a situation of 'heads I win, tails you lose'. In a democracy, the equations are supposed to be transformed towards the public as 'masters' and political representatives as well as administrators as public servants. Nehru, the first Prime Minister, stated and reiterated a number of times, that the Prime Minister is the first servant of the people. Today, citizens are left in wonderment that, while both the elected and appointed public servants have assumed the garb of 'brown-*sahebs*', the "sovereign" people are reduced to subservience, to the status of 'servants', left to 'serve' the so-called public servants. It is not merely appropriation of more than 86 per cent of the revenue contributed by the people, but the people do not get service worth even 14 paise. This unsettling equation between the public and public servants is expressed in terms of people, especially in the "backward" regions such as tribal areas, describing government officials as "sons-in-law of government". Public servants render the assigned service grudgingly, if at all, referring to people as the 'sons-in-law' of the government.

In consonance with the concept of good governance, India has witnessed two phenomena. First is the phenomenal growth of units and layers of the so-called grievance redressal mechanisms – apart from ministerial and administrative 'darbars', face to face or electronically, patronisingly giving 'audience' to the citizens. These grievances of citizens travel up and down, and occasionally across the units, tiers, ministries *et al.* But no government at the centre or in the states, have set up any method of looking at the multitude of grievances and complaints as the best 'feed-back' or Management Information System (MIS) leading to a change in norms, procedures and performance, toning-up administrative machinery so that, similar complaints never repeat. The second phenomenon is the emergence of a plethora of anti-corruption units, tiers and organisations with the Central Vigilance Commission (CVC) as the overarching ombudsman organisation. Yet, corruption has assumed the proportions of a hydra-headed monster, engulfing the expanding network of institutions in the mire of corruption. Today India represents a case of an entire society engulfed in corruption – frighteningly past institutional and individual corruption. Economic liberalisation has transformed the 'art' of corruption. As a consequence, the non-responsive, inaccessible and corrupt institutions of governance have alienated the citizens from the Republic. Such irresponsive process of governance drives the aggrieved citizens and groups to take their problems to institutions outside the frame work of law. Law ceases to take its own course when democrcy is corrupted. Indian Republic has yet to commence its movement towards being a great democracy; it is retarded by the expanding manifestations and growing volume of corruption, earning us a ranking membership among the most corrupt nations. The meaning of democratic discipline, and rule of law have yet to take deep roots in our Republic. Absence of the sense of citizenship, and the associated attributes of pride and patriotism can scorch the efforts of nation-building in India. In this alarming scenario of corruption in governance, the observation of one of the Chief Vigilance Commissioners commending to the citizens the route of Public Interest Litigation (PIL) for containing corruption sounds alarming, indicative of the atrophy of institutions.

In this scenario of a growing sense of withdrawal of citizens from the state – a process of increasing distance between the citizen and the state, and growing distortions in their mutual dispositions and relations – there is an ever-increasing frequency of appeals from the elected representatives as well as administrators to the public for 'public cooperation'. Both political leaders and public administrators have not recognised, that administration cooperating with the public is an essential prerequisite for public cooperating with and participation in the administration. Appreciation and application of this element – cooperating with the pubic – represents a trigger for good governance.

Recognition of the need for 'public cooperation' has to be followed up with the promotion and facilitation of institutions of civil society and methods and processes of engaging the public as a part of enhancing the qualitative viz., responsive and responsible, factors of good governance. For the first four decades the Republic of India had witnessed an adversarial relationship between institutions of governance and the non-governmental development organisations. Then though a phase of assigning tasks by the administrative units to the NGOs as a part of the development projects and process, we now witness an appreciation of the role of NGOs in triggering, managing, monitoring and internalising social development. Yet, even today NGOs are seen selectively through, as adversaries in development in cases such as public hearing of environmental impact assessment of some developmental projects.

Apart from recognising that civil society (peoples) organisations have a critical role to play, political leaders and administrators have to facilitate the working of civil society organisations as a part of legitimisation of change. Once this appreciation comes into play, mechanisms can be innovated, made effective and put in place. Peoples' participation in myriad forms enriches and validates democracy, development and governance. It was in this context even the United Nations had invited the leaders of NGO sector to the global debate on development alongside the heads of states and of governments. Viewed in this background, the much debated, and debatable concept of 'right to information', padded with bureaucratic filters, has to be recast in terms of administrative 'responsibility to 'disclose' and 'inform', contributing to both transparency and accountability, as the two requisites of good governance.

Panchayati Raj institutions, as units of grass-root democracy and participation operating in the proximity of people, can contribute to the objectives of good governance. But, curiously, the elected representatives of the third-tier PRIs are being 'trained' to fit into and 'operate' within the framework of bureaucratic norms, procedures and ethos, instead of preparing them to provide a participative link between the institutions of government and the people. No wonder, the functionaries of PRIs all over the country are frustrated and started assuming a rebellious posture. The two tiers viz. centre and the states must recognise that the PRIs are constitutionally defined and designed as co-equals.

For the teeming millions of Indian citizens, the Constitution means nothing less and nothing more than how and how much it affects their life – physical, social, economic, political and cultural – the quality of their life. Thus, it is the quality of governance that matters, not the promises or provisions of the Constitution, not the avalanche of legislation, and certainly not the extensive and ever-expanding network of administrative machinery. The freedom and dignity of the citizens constitute the corner stone of the Constitution. In the face of an escalation in the cost of administration to the citizen, the benefit of service has touched the rock-bottom; the increasing cost is not matched by performance and productivity, but, more and more of corruption that is proving fatal to the 'Rule of Law', As C. Subramaniam observed, even as the Constitution of India has tried to strike a balance between the citizen and the state, "the citizen is being devalued, the creatures of the dispensation, be it the executive or the legislative, of which ostensibly he is the ultimate arbiter, strut about as demi-gods. In India, of course, unless he wields a knife, or a gun or a bomb the citizen is treated like dirt. The cult of violence could, in this sense, be said to be the consequence of the insensitivity of the State".[22] Citizens tending to take law into their hands, in the face of loss of credibility of State are charged as terrorists, and met by state terrorism.

The increasing onslaught on the basic 'human-rights' of the citizens, in the face of degradation in the quality of life, reflects an admission of failure on the part of state in the translation of constitutional ideals and the delivery of services. The ever increasing violation of human rights also reflects an unsettled relationship between the political and the administrative leadership. "The civil servant is like a well-trained and well-bred horse which by instinct measures its rider. If the rider knows and does his job of reining-in the horse properly, the horse will obey him; if he falters and fumbles, he is bound to fall and bruise himself".[23] This is nowhere better illustrated than in regard to human rights situation, where it is the horse which is found dictating the direction and pace of action.

In place of participative democracy envisioned in the Constitution, India is tending to become a violent society – the citizen and the State are pitted against each other. India is a nation in the making where citizens are alienated from and by the institutions of state. Even if we have the 'finest' of constitutions, unless we have an enabling environment, a constitutional culture, within which it can function, and a (political and administrative) mechanism characterised by commitment to constitutionalism and constitutional goals, we cannot work the Constitution, much less develop the nation.

Issues of privileges and contempt of legislatures and of the Judiciary have long crossed the canons of constitutional democracy. The citizens believe that both the legislatures and the judiciary are not inclined to codify their ever expanding privileges; this tendency amounts to a contempt of the citizens' in any Republic. The privileges, self proclaimed or offered as appeasement, almost in a reciprocal spirit, by the legislative, executive and judicial functionaries are mostly unrelated to their roles and responsibilities. The most vulgar display of these privileges takes place on the streets, and public places in utter contempt of "the people". If we look at the issue from citizens' perspective, excepting the 44th Amendment, constitutional amendments had never contributed to an enlargement of citizens' rights, much less added new rights. Large majorities, centralised political parties without internal democracy, provisions of anti-defection law, crying need for electoral reform, and absence of a process of national consensus based on the vision of the Constitution are some of the factors that are distancing the process and institutions of governance from the citizens.

Indian democracy has turned, almost exclusively, if not entirely 'power-oriented' with the instrumentalities of state assuming an all 'powerful', exclusivist role, the citizen has been excluded from the processes of democracy and reduced to the status of a subject of development. Universal adult suffrage has been provided so as to promote a sense of 'inclusiveness' of every citizen in the mainstream democratic process. We have chosen, in keeping with the times, adult suffrage for this country. I am sure that with the growth of adult education for which we have provided in the Directive Principles, namely, that education must be free and compulsory up to the 14th year for every boy and girl, the unique experiment that we are making in adult suffrage in this country will succeed ere long".[24] But during the life time of the framers of the Constitution, the process of 'exclusion' of citizens has set in, in place of inclusiveness.

The strength of a nation resides, predominantly, in its natural and human resources. Meshing the core strengths of the nation with the desired goals represents the synergy. Freedom and equality should aim at what Glassman has observed as "self-actualising individualism that encourages the individual to make the best of himself or herself".[25] It is towards this end that "no citizen should be so opulent that he can buy another, and none so poor that he is constrained to sell himself".[26] But the Indian Republic reveals precisely this pattern of polarisation that is contra-indicative of a liberal democracy. When naked starvation deaths take place, year after year, the political and bureaucratic leadership attribute such phenomena to health factors, unwittingly revealing the state of health care.

Raja Ram Mohan Roy once remarked that "revolutions never took place when the people had the freedom of expression". Freedom of expression represents a prime characteristic of liberal participative democracy. The paradox of constitutional democracy in India is that the citizens suffered a grievous exclusion from the working of the Constitution, they are not accorded their participatory status even in the exercise of the first national review of the working of the Constitution during the years 1999-2001. Participation provides renewal and nourishment, denial could be fatal.

As the democratising societies are caught in the dilemmas and conflicts arising from liberalisation and globalisation, the civil society has a critical role in arresting and resolving the contradictions of economic restructuring, especially through strengthening political decision-making within a democratic process and people-centered ethos. There is a need for establishing synergic relationship between the political process and civil society. However, in reality, there is an emerging scenario of confrontation between the two with adverse consequences to the processes of democratisation and development. Today even as the United Nations is inviting the civil society to the global conference table on par with the 'official' delegates, national governments have to learn to reclaim and engage the civil society in all spheres of life of the nation.

France, the United Kingdom and the United States of America were held out as the role models, and as the champions of democracy to varying degrees, though the means by, and conditions under which they had evolved as democracies varied widely. India's popular mobilisation towards political freedom, democratic governance, and its constitutional blueprint for social transformation have established, in historical terms, the convergence of ends and means of decolonisation leading to democratisation. The one significant difference between the erstwhile champions of freedom, democracy and human rights on the one hand, and India on the other, is that they were staunch democracies at home, but were colonisers, or traders in people (as slaves). India's freedom movement had acquired the momentum as it was fused with the process of democratiztaion, social reform and the principles of universal and comprehensive human rights. The process of democratisation of the pluralist Indian polity encompassed, in one sweep, equal rights of citizenship, universal adult franchise, and diverse policy norms of affirmative action. The process of democratisation of the Indian polity was not an 'option' but was natural, evolutionary and spontaneous. Thus India was held out as a role model of democratisation during the great wave of decolonisation of the 20th century.

A large number of decolonised communities have not been able to attain a stable state of democracy, and form of governance. These countries, spread across the countinents, are struggling to move towards democratisation, and evolved an esoteric range of mutations and labels of democracy reflecting popular aspirations, and regimes attempting legitimisation. Added to this 'decolonised' countries, struggling to become democratic is the vast numbers and categories of monarchies, sultanates, oligarchies and military dictatorships which are influenced by the universal sweep of democratic norm and process of democratisation. Certainly, the democratic ideal is catching up, but the means (and pace) of democratic transition have not yet been crystalised and institutionalised. In fact, the ends and means debate is raging. The means adopted in bringing about regime-change, as ignition for democracy continue to threaten, and to an extent distort if not destroy, the transition and smooth movement towards people-centred democratisation.

Ends and Means Mix-up

The experiments and experiences of 20th century have crystallised the vision of democracy centering on comprehensive and quantitative human rights, the agenda of human development. Human development has emerged as the goal of economic liberalisation, and of liberal democracy. In deed, democratic 'mode' emerged as the only pathway of sustainable democracy. The ends and means debate has occupied the centre-stage at the United Nations, and even more at the level of communities around the world. Contemporary experiences have also brought out the relative efficacy of the evolutionary processes vis-à-vis the 'external' 'revolutionary' as triggers in promoting democracy.

India as a nascent democracy had suffered an onslaught on its democratic process as a consequence of the internal "emergency" imposed during 1977, paradoxically under the provisions of the democratic Constitution. The umpiring institutions of the Constitution had also failed to stand by the constitutional processes as well as the modes and means of democracy and Rule of law. But, the popular mobilisation, the second mobilisation, with its ethic of freedom movement still afresh, led by the leadership of the civil society had asserted and restored democracy through democratic means. Democratic mode has been reinforced in a manner as to thwart any further recurrence of such a distortion. The Indian experience reveals that democratisation is an internal process, and calls for "socio-legal engineering", a fusion of the ends and means of democracy. When it is perceived and pursued as a "way of life", democracy acquires and internalises a self-corrective process.

What are the means, internal to a polity, that promote the end objective of democratisation in a sustainable manner? Adequate awareness of the quality of life and merits of liberal democracy constitute the seeds of democracy. Such awareness has to be sown taking care of soil conditions and putting in place appropriate and adequate electoral and legislative systems. Leadership which is appreciative and capable of the democratic ethic, moral stamina, and creation of institutions of civil society constitute the most important ingredients – a *sine qua non* for promoting democratic governance and development. One Gandhi, a lone Nelson Mandela, a tenacious Aung San Su Kyi proved to be the fountainhead of democracy.

3.6. Mission Technology

Convergence and synergy

Several national communities that have attained political freedom during the 20th century have learnt from experience that neither ideology nor the form of governance *per se* determine the shape and pace of social transformation. The "developing" world has learnt, the hard way, that (a) the nature and degree of utilisation of science and technology, and (b) mission mode of management of human development represent the two key variables that shape and accelerate development and social transformation.

India's Scientific Policy Resolution as early as 1958, aimed "to secure for the people of the country all the benefits that can accrue from acquisition and application of scientific knowledge". This approach was adopted in the fields of defence, space and agriculture with great success in making rapid strides in the respective fields. But the turning point came when the then Prime Minister Rajiv Gandhi took the initiative, during the year 1985, for the fusion and channelisation of the method and the mission into the process of development in the form of Technology Missions.

The Technology Mission mode had succeeded in making a dent, on the Indian ethos (the 'mind-set') of organisational hierarchy and looking at organisations as a "source of power" instead of perceiving them as a "resource", as a means, in the pursuit of the objectives set out. Institutional cooptation – working together – and synergy constituted the quintessance of the mode of Technology Mission.

The relative success (and the failures) emerging from the Technology Missions reveals that the mission technology works best in situations/organisations where where the leadership is characterised by creativity, conviction and commitment to the mission.

This High-yielding variety of seed was sought to be used for the benefit of "societal" missions. A range of critical spheres such as literacy, health, food, and communications were identified and work initiated. Even as they started showing dramatic results, resistance from the political and administrative culture proved fatal to the innovation[27]. By no means the momentary failure can be attributed to the Technology Mission mode.

Mission-mode is not confined to any specific field of action. It has been applied, adopted and adapted successfully in almost all spheres of human endeavour. The expressions 'missionaries' and 'missionary-zeal' have emerged in the sphere such as philanthropy, education and health-care. There is hardly a corporate organisation that has not formulated and projected a mission-statement, and pursued in action. The emergence and pursuit of India's freedom movement as a vision and its pursuit and achievement reflected, in quintessential terms, the fulfilment of a mission.

India has acquired a place of global pre-eminence in the space, satellite and related spheres by adopting the mission-mode of management. In all these spheres the human factor has emerged as the crucial variable for the success or failure of the mission-mode, the method has emerged successfully in all the instances. It was in this background, the Technology Information Forecasting Assessment Council (TIFAC) was set up in 1996 covering 17 sectors and institutions of national endeavour in the strategic sector with a Projection of Mission 2020.

Assumptions and Core-values of Mission Mode of Management :

There is a widespread perception and assumption that mission-mode of management is not amenable to application in the institutions and processes of governance – especially in the bureaucratic institutions of administration. This perception betrays inadequate appreciation of the Constitution of India which is one of the finest documents of universal human rights, democracy, development and good governance. The misconceptions would also melt away once it is recognised that mission-mode is not a frozen concept or practice, but is situation-specific and hence its success depends upon its creative exploration, adaptation, adoption and application in specific situations.

The dimensions of exploration and innovation in the mission mode of management have been best summed up by APJ Abdul Kalam thus : "Technology denied is technology gained", in the light of experiences when India was denied of emerging technologies by some countries. A challenge can be turned into an opportunity with the adoption of mission-mode of management. There is no possible conflict between ends and means in the mission mode, for the mode demands a fusion of the ends and means. If science and technology[28] are misused or abused by the society, it cannot be blamed on the scientists and technologists.

Convergence, built into the mission-mode of management, contributes to organisational synergy and spin-off benefits. As the mission-mode of management has a wide band of applications, the mode has to be customised to suit specific missions and their respective parameters. As envisioning centres around the people, i.e. translating the dreams have to be 'people-centred' inorder to make them work [with a sense of "do-or-die"], the criticality of the design as a variable is recognised in terms that in the value-chain of a product or a service, design adds value of over 60 per cent. Thus, both the processes of envisioning and converting them into missions are a function of creative leadership. The diverse and often conflicting value-orientations of 'missionaries' vis-à-vis 'administrators' with a rigid set of bureaucratic dispositions are obvious. Impacting of the missionary qualities of leadership becomes a *sine qua non* inorder to be able to induct mission-mode of governance in public administration. Premium on inaction, fear of failure, challenge of innovation and experimentation, blame-game assuming the form of search for scape-goats, hushing-up in place of transparency, all and many of the attributes of bureaucracy, inducted and cultivated from the beginning, often lead to 'who-went-wrong' rather than 'what-went-wrong'. Mission-mode works on the premise that information flow operates like the blood-stream in the human body; it is vital and revitalising. Information-filters, or the premise that 'information is power' could be fatal to the mission-mode of management, whether it is a space-mission or literacy mission.

Empowerment of the involved people, through appropriate and adequate communication channels operates as a multiplier in the mission-mode. In the context of democracy, development and good governance, decentralisation of structures (such as Panchayati Raj Institutions, Cooperatives) and peoples' participation (prioritisation, resource allocation, execution, monitoring and quality assurance) operate as multipliers of development, apart from promoting trust, accountability and self reliance.

Mission-mode sets out explicitly stated and shared paremeters, contra-inidcators as well as tolerance limits that would facilitate on-line monitoring, feedback and course correction. In the ultimate analysis, mission-mode of management promotes cooptation, convergence and synergy.

Missions are geared to the vision of a community, a nation and humanity as a whole – they are geared to a given set of goals and objectives. Creative leadership, exploration and innovation are the vital forces, sourced from dedication and devotion, (best described as *Shraddha* and *Bhakti*, in the Indian context). Envisioning leading to formulation of a mission is not utopian. India and many countries have demonstrated mission-mode of management, in several spheres. Mission formulation not only transcends but, in fact integrates seemingly diverse concerns of society – liberal democracy, economic development and good governance – into a unified mission. Viewed from the stand-point of the Constitution of India the political, the economic, the social-cultural, and the governance processes are not independent of each other, they are not sequential either, but integral and concurrent inorder to move the nation in the direction of the Constitutional vision.

Mission mode demands complementarity of roles and commonality of objectives – every single unit in its own place, each one as important as any other. It is only when all the actors appreciate, equally well, this complementarity (supported by conviction and commitment), convergence and synergy take place leading to the fulfilment of the mission. The debate that often surfaces in the form of 'individuals versus systems' has no place in the mission-mode where both are critical and have to operate with the highest degree of congruence. So also hierarchy, controls based on power and authority operating as 'checks' and 'balances' have no place in a mission-mode of management. All systems and subsystems have to operate, fine-tuned to an over arching set of mission objectives, mission parameters and on-line monitoring. Targets related to time-management (in terms of milestones) quality-standards, least cost and goals achieved (objectives fulfilled) represent some of the parameters for the mission-mode of management.

References

1. Raj Bahadur, The Constituent Assembly, ibid p. 142.
2. The Constitution and the Constituent Assembly Salient features of the Constitution Achievements of the Constituent Assembly M Ananthasayanam Ayyangar, November 18, 1949, pp. 151.
3. The Constitution and the Constituent Assembly Salient features of the Constitution Achievements of the Constituent Assembly M Ananthasayanam Ayyangar, November 18, 1949, pp. 152.
4. The Constitution and the Constituent Assembly Salient features of the Constitution The Draft Constitution Dr. B.R. Ambedkar, November 4, 1948, pp. 114 & 115.

5. The Constitution and the Constituent Assembly Salient features of the Constitution Reply to the Debate Dr. B.R. Ambedkar, November 25, 1949, pp. 176.

6. G.R.S. Rao, Managing Change in Police Organisations, Journal of the SVP National Police Academy, Jul-Dec 2003 pp. 12-19.

7. The Constitution and the Constituent Assembly Salient features of the Constitution Reply to the Debate Dr. B.R. Ambedkar, November 25, 1949, pp. 177.

8. The Constitution and the Constituent Assembly Salient features of the Constitution. The Draft Constitution Dr. B.R. Ambedkar, November 4, 1948, pp. 121 & 122.

9. *Ibid* p. 122.

10. B.R. Ambedkar, The Constitution and the Constituent Assembly : Salient Features of the Constitution. Reply to the Debate Nov. 25, 1949 p. 177.

11. For a detailed discussion ref. GRS Rao, Productivity in Government in Productivity Vol. 31 No. 1'Apr – Jun, 1990 pp. 86 - 92.

12. GRS Rao, Impact of Constitutional Amendments on the Federal Character of India. Round Table on the Constitution of India, RIIPAA Hyderabad, 1989, pp. 1-19.

13. Nani A. Palkhivala, Six Fatal Mistakes of Free India, Bhavan's Journal Jan. 31, 2003, p. 147.

14. HVR Iyengar, Administration of India; A Historical Review 1967.

15. B.R. Ambedkar Ibid p. 122.

16. Mahatma Gandhi Quit India Resolution, Indian National Congress, Karachi 1942.

17. Jawaharlal Nehru, Constitution and Constituent Assembly Ibid pp. 56-57.

18. Lok Nayak Jaya Prakash Narayan. Quoted in GRS Rao Dynamics of Democratisation, in Legislative Support Services in Asia, SOCORRO L. Reyes (ed) CRTS Manila 1994 pp. 35-63.

19. Public Interest Litigation by the Peoples' Union for Civil Liberties, HINDU, Hyderabad, November 22, 2001.

20. Dr. S. Radhakrishnan, An Appeal for Concord : Constitution and Constituent Assembly, Ibid, p. 60.
21. GRS Rao, An Appraisal of Tribes Advisory Councils under the Constitution of India. (®Report) ASCI-MSW, GOI 1995.
22. Subramaniam, letter from the President, Bhavan's Journal Apil 15, 1991 p. 10.
23. C. Subramaniam, letter from the President, Bhavan's Journal Dec. 31, 1990 p. 10.
24. The Constitution and the Constituent Assembly : Salient features of the Constitution Achievements of the Consembly, M. Ananthasayanam Ayyangar, Nov. 18, 1949 p. 153.
25. Glasman, Ronald M. The New Middle Class and Democracy in Global Perspective, New York, NY. St Martins Press 1997, p. 236.
26. Rcusseau, Jean Jaques. On the Social Contact Trans. Judith R Masters, New York Ny. St Martius Press 1978.
27. For a detailed review and appraisal see : Technology Missions by GRS Rao, Rajiv Gandhi Formation, New Delhi 1995.
28. For a detailed review of Accountability of the profession of Science and Technology, see PM Bhargava in Accountability of Public Institutions (ed) GRS Rao, RIIPAA Hyderabad 1991 pp. 141-162.

4

PROGRESSION - REGRESSION

The Quality of Change

The Preamble and the Directive Principles of State Policy set out the substance of, and the road map for democratic, social transformation. Responding to some criticism that the Directive Principles are only pious declarations, Dr. Ambedkar maintained that "whoever captures power will not be able to do what he likes with it. In the exercise of it, he will have to respect these, he may not have to answer for their breach in a court of law. But he will certainly have to answer for them before the electorate at election time",[1] the peoples' court. The Preamble and the Directive Principles are set to operate as the beacon light to the process of public policy making in the country. Every step taken should conform to the spirit of this normative direction of the Constitution. The question arises if we are moving in the direction of the parameters set, and if we are doing so, whether the pace is adequate to fulfil the promise, and clear the backlog, or we are adding to the aggregation as the 'lost agenda'.

The discussions in the Consembly consensually reinforced the design parameters of the Constitution on the human dimension of development. This is reflected by scholars on development, in quintessential terms of universal humanistic values rather than in narrow, segmented techno-economic parameters. Thus, viewed one way, five core principles emerge "which stand inseparably together". They are : (1) Man as the end objective of development – which is therefore, to be judged by what it does to him. (2) Recognition of the twin dimensions that human beings feel at home with the process of development in which they become the subject as well as the object. (3) Development of the collective personality of man in which he finds his richest experience. (4) Participation as the core of democratic ethic, and (5) Self-reliance as the expression of man's faith in his own abilities. In the ultimate analysis, thus, the substance of democracy and development are inseparable. The facets of such an integrated development got reflected in the vision of the Consembly as an echo of the aspirations of the people. These humanist values get reflected in the quality of life of the community, at the collective as well as the individual levels.

Just three days before his assassination Mahatma Gandhi said : "the Indian National Congress has won political freedom, but it has yet to win economic, social and moral freedoms. These are harder than political freedom, because they are constructive and not exciting and not spectacular – if the Congress engages in the ungainly skirmish for power, it will find one fine morning that it is no more".[2] It was a summation of the national agenda, the socio-economic substance of political freedom; the urgency reflected in terms of 'perform or perish'.

The fulfilment of the agenda of economic, social and moral freedoms, interdependent as they are, can be measured on a scale of progression-stagnation-regression over a period of time. In reality, no society can endure 'stagnation' for long, for it leads to a slide-down on the dimension of regression. Thus, social transformation can be measured essentially on a two-dimensional scale of 'Progression-Regression'. The fulfilment of constitutional vision of India is a function, in aggregated holistic terms, of three processes viz., (1) nature of integration of democracy and development, (2) convergence of the economic 'heights' and the social 'sights' set out, while ensuring that no 'contra-indicators' emerge, and (3) the nature and quality of socio-legal engineering so as to promote and sustain transformation of the pluralist society into an integrated nation with the citizens experiencing pride of citizenship. All the three processes are interdependent, and in the aggregate shape the largest democracy move on the dimension of progression towards becoming a great vibrant democracy maintaining a dynamic equilibrium. The alternative is not stagnation but degrees slide into a turbulent and a violent society, at war with itself, on the dimension of 'Regression'.

4.1. Integration of Democracy and Development

The Constitution has carved out the vision of India in a manner as to integrate democracy and development not in terms of "means" and an "end", but as the twin processes with a reciprocal relationship. Democracy and development (*Sarva Sammati, Sarva Hita* in the best interest of all, and *Sarvodaya,* unto the last) have been fused to such a fine degree that there is no differentiation in terms of 'means' and the 'ends'. The means, i.e., democratisation has been seen as an integral part of the end objective, the multi-faceted human development. In the reality of Indian democracy, the first five decades have witnessed segregation, and a failure in the integration of democracy and development. The consequence is that both the processes have been fragmented and distorted, in diverse manner. India has made significant strides, but what remains to be done is formidable.

In the constitutional architecture and blueprint, It is only when the two processes are fused together and placed on the constitutional trajectory that they would contribute to human development, the quality of life of the citizens, marking the progression. However, as macro 'development' has taken the measure of GDP, democracy and quality of life have remained mal-nourished. As we have not succeeded in fusing the two, mere increases in GDP has led to Gross Social Conflict (GSC) as a consequence. The pattern of democratic development is projected in Illustration 4.1.

The manner of our engagement and preoccupation with the economy of the country, has not contributed to 'nation-building', promotion of citizenship and a sense of pride in nationalism. The unintended consequences are the fragmentation of the society, and fracturing of the Republic. As every conceivable social 'trauma' has been converted into a political 'drama', the legitimacy and credibility of the process and character of constitutional democratic society has suffered incalculably. Gross Social Conflict (GSC) being witnessed in India represents a contra-indicator of democratic-development. India seems to have sailed through the dangerous decades, but not yet reached a stable state in the process of promoting continuity and change. Attaining and sustaining a stable state is a function of harmonisation of democracy and development.

It is not just development but the process of development that has acquired primacy towards the end of 20th century on a global scale. Sustainable development reflects the process parameters. The most commonly used description of sustainability was defined by the World Commission on Environment and Development (the Brundtland Commission) thus: "development that meets the needs of the present without compromising the ability of future generations to meet their own needs". Sustainability of development is based on the interdependence of environmental, social and economic sub-systems. Sustainable development, that which sustains equality and equity, emerges from the empowerment of people, and recognition of universal humanism. Thus it strengthens democratic process. Sustainability of development is based on fulfilment of human needs such as clean air and water, food and shelter, education and productive employment. Development becomes sustainable through public involvement in exploring local solutions to environmental and developmental problems.

ILLUSTRATION 4.1

DEMOCRATIC DEVELOPMENT

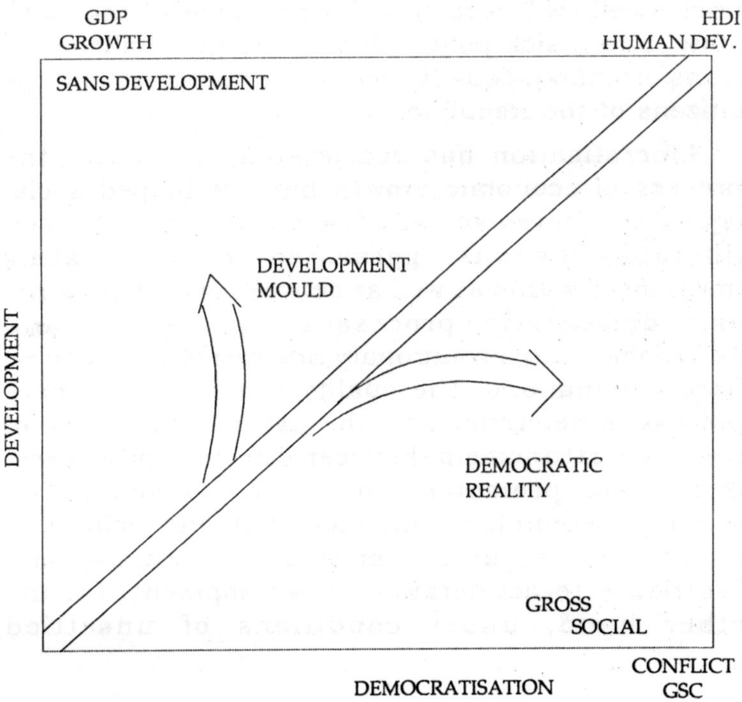

A wide range of inter-related factors have been identified as responsible for the shortfall in our performance as a Republic. These factors can be categorised into six clusters viz. (a) illiteracy, religious, and other prejudices (b) lack of conviction and commitment towards the constitutional goals on the part of political leaders, the absence of a national outlook, inefficient leadership, erosion of ethical values, corruption, judicial subservience to the executive; nexus between politicians and the bureaucracy, and lack of commitment on the part of administrators; (c) concentration of power in the hands of the state, lack of access to justice, utter lack of accountability, public extravagance, single dominant party at center for long years, and party control over elected representatives reinforced by the anti-defection legislation; (d) distorted priorities; (e) high growth rate of population, and (f) inert attitude of intelligentia. These factors of regression allowed unchecked, will lead to a further slide of the 'soft-state' into a sick-polity. Herein lies the challenge of transformation, equally, before the managers and the citizens of the Republic.

Liberalisation has accelerated, no doubt, the process of economic growth but not helped social equity or an even spread of democratisation. In fact, liberalisation has aggravated the preexisting imbalances within as well as between growth patterns and democratic processes. Democracy and development are evolutionary processes; there are no fixed destinations. The quality of this evolutionary process is determined by the nature and degree of constant attunement between the two processes. Democracy promotes innovation; consequently, science, technology, management and economic activity flourish under democratic conditions, and contribute to acceleration of development. On the other hand, under conditions of unsettled democracy, development could create unsettling social conditions. It can be hypothesise that enhancement in the quality of democracy, decentralise structures and participative processes would smoothen the imbalances within the development process, and will thus help absorb the process of liberalisation. It is the 'process' that would help contain regression and promote progression.

4.2. Economic Heights and Social Sights

An overview of the patterns of economic growth and social change during the first five decades suggests that the movement of the two has been at variance with each other as indicated in Illustration 4.2.

ILLUSTRATION 4.2

PATTERNS OF ECONOMIC GROWTH AND SOCIAL CHANGE

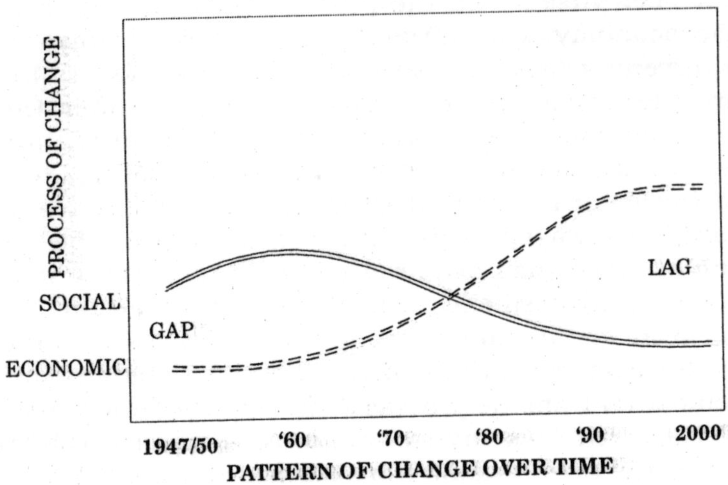

The patterns of economic growth and social change can be noticed, broadly, as falling into three phases : 1950-70; 1970-85 and 1985-2000. The two processes were neither fine-tuned, nor found to be moving towards a convergence. On the other hand, the 'gap' between the economic and social conditions at the starting line have grown into an expanding 'lag' between the macro economic growth and the micro social condition which can be described as social regression. Many factors can be identified as being responsible for this growing lag. Some of the more prominent factors are the distortions in the processes of democracy (of power, of short sighted vision among the political leadership, inadequacies in the management of financial resources and methods of planning, and dilution of the values of liberal democracy as inherited from the freedom movement). The most recent and dominant factor for this 'lag' is the loss of sight of the national and social objectives of economic liberalisation set in motion during the early nineties. The values of liberal democracy have not been fused with the process of liberalisation of the economy. Of course there is a whole range of intervening factors responsible for this 'lag', which are identified in the ensuring analysis under the caption 'socio-legal engineering'. GDP orientation has been accentuated unrelated to the HDI, leading to increasing levels of GSC. If the present trend continues, we will register rapid growth no doubt, for our economy has acquired self-sustaining and self-accelerating resilience. But, it will aggravate the lag between growth and development processes, which in substance means, distancing the substance of democracy from the process of development. Our 1947 'Tryst With Destiny', could then take a fatal or 'fatalistic' turn, arising from the back lash of GSC.

Some 'indigent' sections of the population, who do not have even an awareness of their citizenship, and of our Constitution, resign to their 'fate', attributing their inhuman levels of existence to 'destiny'; a sign of withdrawal and self exclusion from the democratic process. The second category attribute the distortions in social change to the working of the Constitution. The third category of people attribute the deteriorating conditions of their life to the provisions of the Constitution. Attributing such deterioration to the inadequacies in the Constitution, people have started demanding a second, more 'radical' Constitution; a second Republic. They do not see any sanctity attached to the Constitution, for, it has not lent any meaning to their life.

Progress, *Abhyudaya,* is possible only when material growth contributes to social welfare. "I will give you a talisman. Whenever you are in doubt... Recall the face of the poorest and the weakest man and ask yourself, if the step you contemplate is going to be of any use to him. Will he gain anything by it? Will it restore him a control over his own life and destiny? In other-words, will it lead to *Swaraj* for the hungry and spiritually starving millions? Then you will find your doubts melting away",[3] observed Gandhi. The Indian economy has made significant strides since Independence, aided by a 'planned' economic development. But it has not benefitted the bottom-rung, leading to exclusion instead of the intended norm of inclusion.

The advent of 'political freedom' had seen India, paradoxically, moving around with a 'begging bowl' in such a manner that many an observer stated that India can never become self-sufficient in the production of food-grains to feed its hungry millions. But, in less than three decades, the nation has registered, *inter alia,* a Green Revolution and a White Revolution. We have attained not merely self-sufficiency but also built-up sizable buffer stocks. We have been able to absorb shocks arising from the cycle of droughts and floods. We could not only export, but also go to the aid of the other democratising countries in meeting scarcity conditions.

Our industrial infrastructure has been substantially expanded, and economy has registered significant growth and diversification. As a nascent democracy, we have risen from the bottom, to become one among the top ten of the economies. As a vast country, with an expanding economy, our economy has attained a continental character, able to meet the ever-diversifying demands, absorb such international shocks as the oil crises, and the pressures of war, and yet registered commendable growth. The chain of research and development institutions has helped considerably in evolving innovative solutions to problems and in absorbing new technologies, thus contributing to the modernisation of both the agricultural and industrial sectors. An overview of our economy suggests that if we look at our growth *per se*, we have attained great heights, "commanding heights", inspite of a variety of constraints.

In the sphere of economic and industrial development, at the starting line, democratic India had three broad alternative paths viz. Gandhian *Swadeshi*, Nehruvian socialism (with an accent on the state controlling and "commanding" the economy), or free economy propounded by Rajagopalachari. Due to a variety of historical factors, the nation was put on the track of a 'socialistic-pattern' of development, a mix, if not a synthesis, of all the three options and models. It can hardly be challenged, wrote Nehru, that "in the context of the modern world, no country can be politically and economically independent, unless it is highly industrialise. An industrially backward country will prompt aggressive tendencies of the more developed countries. This control will inevitably upset our economy. Thus an attempt to build up a country's economy largely on the basis of small scale industries is doomed to failure. It will not solve the basic problems of the country or maintain freedom, nor will it fit in with world framework, except as a colonial appendage". Thus, the foundations for 'public' sector , and for large-scale in preference to the small-scale sector were laid by Nehru. The unfortunate aspect was that the foundations of public sector were laid in terms of 'Public versus Private' rather than in complementary terms. In tune with the Nehruvian prescription that the "means of production should be socially owned and controlled for the benefit of society as a whole", the Five Year Plans of development were designed. "One comes inevitably to the conclusion that a rapid expansion of the economic and social responsibilities of the state will alone be capable of satisfying the legitimate expectations of the people. This need not involve complete nationalisation of the means of production or elimination of private agencies. It does mean, however, a progressive widening of the public sector and a reorientation of the private sector to the needs of a planned economy".[4]

We aimed at, in Jawaharlal Nehru's words, "an egalitarian society, in which equal opportunities are provided to every member for self-expression and self-fulfilment and an adequate minimum of a civilise standard of life is assured to each member so as to make the attainment of this equal opportunity a reality . . .". However, what was witnessed is that a small section of society controlling and enjoying the fruits of growth, with an ever increasing 'parallel' economy operating alongside growing poverty, displacement and disruption of backward 'communities' in the name of development of backward 'areas', glaring discrimination between the organise and unorganise labour, industrial strife in place of participative management, and an unsustainable level of consumer grievances more from public sector monopoly services. The enumeration can go on. The objectives of social development have not been consciously and organically linked to the mode of economic growth, but were allowed, by default and remain as one of its by-products.

Ever increasing black money (often referred to as parallel economy), and economic offences in the face of a bulging poverty line; glaring differences in the standards of treatment in an ambience of public versus private sector industries, extensive protection to 10 to 15 per cent of workers in the organise sector in the face of exploitative equations in the unorganised sector; the process of neutralisation of cost of living index to numerically insignificant minority at the cost of the majority of citizens, the demos suffering from a deteriorating standard of living, disincentives to growth of small scale sector adversely affecting self reliant employment potential, and many other such consequences of policies and practices reflected the distortions of development. The Constitutional Directives in regard to right to work, humane working conditions, living wage, opportunities for the enjoyment of leisure, represent an agenda that has been lost sight of. An overview of India's experiments and experiences have revealed that the political, economic, social and cultural facets of democracy and development have been pursued in isolation. This dynamic of democratic development has been and continues to be neglected even after it was recognised.

The Constitution has created the political base for democracy in terms of one person one vote. Yet it has not led to the creation of material conditions whereby 40 to 50 per cent of population who continue to exist and survive below the 'poverty-line' are lifted to the base-line of citizenship. Some macro material conditions have changed, as illustrated by the production levels of foodgrains and G.D.P. Famines may have faded, but deaths due to starvation and malnutrition persist, consistently in some pockets. The basic needs of health, education and drinking water are also persisting with dead-lines that have defied fulfilment. They are being adjusted constantly in tune with the competitive populism of political process and fluctuating frequency of the electoral cycles.

We have not allowed ourselves to be influenced adequately by the constitutional directives towards employment especially in the rural-tribal India. The process and pattern of 'growth' are not able to meet, but are only contributing to the ever increasing problems of unemployment in the rural economy (with its attendant social consequences), generating 'push' factors of an ever increasing 'distress-migration', in the form of 'refugees of development'. It is not that we have not been able to innovate initiatives such as PURA and Mission Technology to meet the backlog of development inorder to fuse growth with social justice and equity.

Our record of "planned development" suggests that we respond to the sections of population that organise themselves, and resort to agitational mode, that too, only after antagonistic and hostile dispositions are generated. This phenomenon was vividly demonstrated by a trade-union leader when he told a manager : "what is it that you have given? Whatever we got we fought for and won". To top it all, rural unrest emerging from 'developmental by-pass', is perceived both by the centre and the states as a law and order problem. The Constitution has yet to succeed in inspiring and impacting our developmental ethos. The worsening situation in respect of poverty and inequities provided the compulsion for accelerated economic liberalisation. But, inadequate attunement of economic reform to the promise and fulfilment of the Constitution represents the gap between the constitutional vision and the conviction of national leadership a distortion represents the deviance in the management of the Constitution. This managerial distortion is reflected in the neglect and delayed response to the national requirements of inducting technologies to promote higher productivity and value-addition in the agricultural sector, right from seed-to-grain, seed-to-vegetable, seed-to-fruit and milk production. The phenomena of growing unemployment, distress-migration, and unprecedented occurrence of suicides among the farming communities emerged as the grave consequences of managerial deficiencies.

Observing that many of the reform measures were not rooted in, and suited to the Indian genius, George Monbiet [6] reflected that aid was being used as a tool for recolonisation through privatisation. Economic Liberalisation was pursued in a manner that the State ceased to be a trustee of natural resources. Reflecting on the experiments and experiments especially in Andhra Pradesh state, Monbiet observed that the state was being used as a laboratory for mass-privatisation, and public-private partnership in setting up hospitals, in the name of restructuring, dispossessing a large number of people and thus contributing to poverty aggravation instead of alleviation.

The advances made in the sphere of science and technology represent the silver lining of development in India. India produced PARAM super computer; launched its own satellites becoming one of only six nations in the world. What is more, India has announced that it can, and plans to, land a man on the moon by 2010. India has the world's largest working population (15 – 45 years) of 60 crores (600 millions). However, we have not matched our attainments with our needs and potential. The 'deficit' in performance becomes more glaring when compared to performance of Indians away from home. This deficit can only be explained in terms of values and attitudes, shaping the work ethic, measured in terms of 'motivational gap'.

The Gandhian model of '*Gram Swaraj*' and '*Swadeshi*' as the strategies for social transformation may not have been found appropriate and thus not acceptable. But, who can ever dispute the goals of *Antyodaya* and *Sarvodaya* as the substance of economic and socio-cultural freedom representing the fulfilment of political freedom? Citizenisation of people represents the constitutional minima, and the starting-point of the arduous journey of social transformation. In comparative terms, in the comity of nations, India stands 55th in Human and Income Poverty Index (HPI); and at 115th with reference to Human Development Index (HDI) – a distressingly low level, especially in the absence of any institutionalised provision for social security. Using the National Sample Survey (NSS) estimates, Gupta suggests that between 1990-91 and 1998, the percentage of people below poverty line (BPL) has increased from 35.11 to 43.01[7]. It has increased to 43.20 in Government of India (GOI) Survey of Poverty (May 2000).

Suggesting the need to formulate a more comprehensive set of indicators of human development and welfare, M.S. Swamiathan proposes 11 clusters of such markers.[5] They are : (1) nutrition security (2) water security (3) literacy and 'technocracy' (4) health security (5) shelter (6) ecological security (7) livelihood security (8) energy security (9) gender-equity (10) folk, classical and modern art, culture, music and drama, and (11) technological leap-froging. Economic and social security constitute vital ingredients of the internal security of a nation.

We are sliding down the various targets set and constantly shifting targeted dates with alarming consistency – such as drinking water for all by 1980, health for all by 2000. People are waging 'civil wars' for drinking water; states are formulating plans to deploy 'water-police', and are locked-up in inter-state disputes. There is not only a criminal waste of water but equally of the time of the Judiciary due to inter-state legal battles. Instead of promoting national integration, people are massed-up on inter-state borders, generating hostile attitudes and hostilities. A clear case of political drama in the face of social trauma.

It is estimated that 20.0 per cent of the population enjoys 80.0 per cent of goods and services in India, leaving the balance of 20.0 per cent to be shared by 80.0 per cent of the citizens – a skewed pattern that negates the concept of distributive justice. India seems to have two seasons of human misery, year after year, the seasons of floods and drought. Death and destruction are not only reduced to statistics, but more often than not relief is politicised, bureaucratised, corrupted and thus dehumanised. Two distinct distortions appear to have crept into our concept of a welfare state, and its operationalisation. In the name of development, especially of the weaker sections, (including SCs, STs), we have promoted dependence on 'doles', rather than self-reliance and self-respect emerging from a sense of pride in citizenship. Even a cursory review of the 'development' of Scheduled Tribes reveals how much damage "we" have inflicted on 'them'. Their status, (viewed from many angles) would have been better today had our 'developmental' process ignored them, left them untouched. The issue is not one of their 'development', but the inadequate and faulty strategies adopted and the nature change brought about in the name of development. As B.R. Ambedkar has observed, "Political democracy cannot last unless there lies at the base of it social democracy. What does social democracy mean? It means a way of life which recognises liberty equality and fraternity as the abiding principles of liberal democracy . . . . to divorce one from the other is to defeat the very purpose of democracy".[8] The unredeemed pledge enshrined in the Constitution in regard to dignity of individual has led to an erosion of faith in the state.

Another distortion of the welfare state is the bureaucratisation of welfare. It is conceded even by the exceptionally well meaning bureaucrats that bureaucracy, as it is obtaining in India today, with no signs of reform in sight, is not equipped to deliver social services, much less promote social welfare. Even worse, most of the allocations are going towards the costs of administration, that has grown into a white elephant.

At the advent of political freedom, the whole nation was in 'gratitude' to the founding fathers; within a few decades the nation found itself 'in debt' due to the successors of the founding fathers. The successors are also found to have reduced 'multiplier' factors, such as education, by keeping as many as 400 million child-labour below the age of 14 as illiterates), Judith R. Masters stated that "no children should be so opulent that he can buy another, and none so poor that he is constrained to sell himself".[9] One wonders whether she was reflecting on the Indian reality. "The choice is not between the market mechanism and government intervention . . . but between policies that combine equity and rapid capital accumulation, on the one side, and persistent inequality and inefficiency on the other. The Post 1991 New Economic Policy reforms have taken a few tentative steps to reduce inefficiency, they have done little to reduce inequality".[10]

New Economic Policy was adopted primarily inorder to accelerate growth which is a necessary prerequisite but does not automatically lead to social development. On the other hand, it has been recognised the world over, that liberalisation could lead to (a) weakening of a nation-state, (b) dormancy and failure of the mediating institutions between the individual and the state such as family, church, voluntary associations, neighbourhoods and sub-cultures, (c) a diminition of the prospects of individuals controlling their own lives, (d) a pervasive sense of helplessness on the part of hapless citizens, and (e) a growing influence of business interests over the government. All these features emerging in India in an accentuated manner since the 1990 economic liberalisation represent contra-indicators to the process of social development that the Constitution of India enunciates; Indian state has not taken adequate and appropriate measures to keep these contra-indicators under check.

Socio-Legal Engineering

The term 'nation' connotes people living together in a specified territory and united by the ties of community of language, race and politics. Dr. Ambedkar wondered : "how can people, divided into several thousands of castes, be a nation"? Since, all people in the polyglot are not equal in India, special provisions were made inorder to even-out these differences and to make every individual feel and experience "equality" of citizenship, as an integral part of nation-building. The constitutional vision set out India on the path of democratisation, reflecting a set of liberal values such as (a) mellowing the onslaught of capitalism, (b) recognition of diversity in unity, (c) all individual 'freedoms' unified into a collective freedom, and (d) harmony in place of social strife, inorder to protect and promote nationalism.

Social reform was initiated as an integral part of the freedom movement. The backlog encompassed evils such as untouchability, *Sati*, dowry, child-labour, diversity in customs and practices emerging from cultural pluralism. The communal factor, accentuated as a backlash of partition, may be added to this 'backlog'. The freedom movement succeeded in focussing and promoting awareness among the people, of some of these issues. Social change in regard to long-standing beliefs, prejudices and practices cannot be brought about by the promulgation of ordinances, but calls for socio-legal engineering supported by distributive policies. As a follow-up of the constitutional promise 'enabling' legislation has been adopted; but the process of social engineering has suffered several and severe distortions at the hands of the state. In itself it reflected the assumption that the state is not the best instrument for promoting social engineering. True transformation called for a process of popular mobilisation and a social movement. It was for this reason Mahatma Gandhi said that promoting social democracy and economic freedom was lot more challenging than securing political freedom. And with this in view, he had suggested converting the INC into a social service organisation.

The shift in the focus of political process from a mass movement to an instrument of 'power' focussed on electoral process had brought about a radical change in the role of politics. Before the other forces of social reform could organise and step in, the partisan political process found the backlog of social agenda handy for competitive populism. This mix-up of social agenda and partisan pursuit of power, had proved fatal to the process of socio-legal engineering. The problem cannot be seen in either black or white, there are shades of grey. Education, employment and urbanisation have contributed to the melting away of caste as a phenomenon. Competitive populism, electoral politics, and double standards, the media projection vis-à-vis private prejudices and attendant practices of political leaders have not arrested the dilution of caste but in fact contributed to the resurrection and accentuation of such prejudices and practices. Partisan political processes are reflected in the selection of candidates for electoral positions, and composition of cabinets. The virus had spread from the political to the other sectors of the society such as appointments to positions of Vice Chancellors of universities and as members of the Judiciary. All over India caste in its myriad manifestations had been accorded a heavy weightage. What is of significance, negative though, is that caste credentials are projected as 'legitimate' demands with matching responses from the partisan political bosses. Administration did not lag behind.

Instead of servicing social transformation, with a citizen-centric mode of governance, the administration had retained its colonial focus and modus. During the initial decades it had been referred to by the society as he "change-agents", but, soon, very soon, it had given up the new nomenclature and had restored, with great ease, its own erstwhile classical bureaucratic character – a parallel power-center with added flair. The self-centered and self-serving bureaucracy not only impeded the democratic empowerment of people, but, added negative values of corruption on its own terms as well as in collaboration with the corrupt in the political system. That this collaborative exploitation had acquired the character of a 'nexus' is officially documented, experienced and suffered by the people. The only alibi that administrators hold out, a process of ratinoalisation is that the society is corrupt and that a society gets the administration that it deserves. The constitutional role assigned, the solemn swearing they undertake at the time of entry, and that as functionaries with a lead status they cannot take umbrage under the pretest that the "society is corrupt". Reform is anathema, for it hurts their interests of power, corruption, and career prospects; hurts even more their anathema for public service. Socio-legal engineering is thus out of the bounds of bureaucracy. No wonder, corruption has not only decelerated but also faulted the process of social transformation, and debilitated the prospects of good governance. When the government itself fails democracy with total disdain, the ills of corporate-governance cannot be found fault with. Thanks to liberalisation of economies, corruption is blamed as a global phenomenon. With increasing distances and growing distortions in the relations between the people on one side and the political and administrative subsystems on the other, it is not only that social agenda is lost sight of, but more critically, their relations are turning sour, adversary and hostile. The political paries explain it away, in an attempt to rationalise, as "anti-incumbancy" rather than as a vote against malfunctioning which is the common denominator of all political parties. The hostility against the administration has now assumed the form of Public Interest Litigation (PIL). PIL can't be the mode of democratic social transformation; it can, and in fact has diverted the political and administrative processes towards judicialisation. Judiciary cannot take on the load of PIL, nor the role of political/administrative institutions. As a consequence of its attempts to correct the malfunctioning of governance, Judicial activism, both wittingly and unwittingly, assumed the forms of intervention, 'extremism' et al with the attendant role-relationships as between the different instrumentalities of state assuming adversary form, building up into conflict and confrontation. When the constitutional architecture of complementarity of roles and commonality of goals got destroyed, the constitutional agenda of social transformation is impeded, socio-legal engineering becomes dysfunctional.

The institutional conflict-mode gets handy, especially for the political leaders as an alibi for non-performance, and projection of unrelated aspects such as 'presidential' versus 'parliamentary' democracy, Judicial reform, electoral reforms, inter-se immunities and privileges, and checks and balances. The slide is revealed by instances such as the decision of the Supreme Court to review its own judgement barring strikes by government employees can send wrong signals to the public servants, that can prove dangerous to democracy.

In the given complexity of the situation, there appears an agreement on experiments and experiences that : (a) the constitutional measures did not work in the manner they had been designed, leading to, (b) increase in the degree of frustration, (c) rampant corruption (d) emergence of creamy layers impeding the percolation of benefits, (e) vested interests in backwardness, (f) reverse discrimination, and (g) exceptions swallowing the rule. Literacy and education as multipliers for sustainable social development had given way to quantitative approaches, without a correlation to qualitative parameters.

Regional imbalances in the standards and quality of life have been taken cognizance of by the Constitution, and policy directives provided to remedy backwardness. But the range of programs and modes of implementation had led to consequences, directly opposite to the objectives intended. It was a case of the development process leading to social degradation and disruption, as evidenced by contra-indications. The negative impact on the rural / backward areas pales into insignificance when compared to the impact on tribal communities for whose benefit special provisions and directives were incorporated in the Constitution, and special institutions such as Tribes Advisory Councils (TACs). Protective measures such as a direct constitutional role and responsibility assigned to the Governors of states and to the President of India did not work.

Jawaharlal Nehru brought out explicitly the three policy alternatives available, and the constitutionally sanctified choice in regard to protection of the interests and cultural identities of tribal communities while promoting their welfare. The three options that he had identified were (a) protection of their cultural identity and interests of the tribal communities while delivering the benefits of development as a part of promoting their welfare, (b) total integration into the mainstream so that there will be no more identifiable tribal communities, and (c) leaving them untouched, in isolation, as the third policy option. Nehru made it abundantly clear that the Constitution envisions a policy of protection of their cultural identity and yet delivery of the benefits of development, especially those in regard to education, medicare and livelihood. In reality, what happened to the tribal communities has been the worst blend of the three possibilities.[11]

Social distances are growing as the pre-existing prejudices are getting accentuated and hardened. Inadequate appreciation of the dynamics of management of change is leading to a regression of the social order; occasionally there is a facile argument that such a reversal is in tune with the dynamics of change. A quintessentially secular constitution, as explained explicitly in the Consembly, has been amended merely to affix the label of "secular" leading to extensive political rhetoric and contrived conflict. While the rhetoric itself has generated heat without throwing light, the issue has been dragged to the court of the Judiciary which only stated that the expression defies a precise description and has yet to be defined precisely. The issue is not as to what religion is doing to politics, but as to what politics is doing to religion.

Given recognition to the fact that secularism is not irreligion, or anti- religion, religion has a potential and positive contribution to make as an 'equaliser' of social relations and political equations. But, the current Indian brand of 'secularism' is a dangerous mix of partisan politics and religious fanaticism creating a vertical social schism. We need to segregate the two in the first place, before we start moving on the secular path. Religious discourse, which has the potential to take people to great spiritual heights, is being abused to debunk democracy and social transformation in India.

On the ground, India has a variety of political parties based on religion; religion is everywhere, occasionally assuming the menacing proportions of communalism. Religious conversion takes place, on a large scale, purely emerging from poverty, for a paltry sum of Indian Rs.500/-. Religious subversion fetches a better price than that. Political debate focuses attention so exclusively on secularism that no party looks at caste-based political parties and processes that could be as disastrous, if not more, because there is an ever increasing number, (several hundreds) of castes, than a handful of religions. The partisan political process in India today has placed caste on the same axis as if religion.

While the material conditions have not moved in the positive direction, in consonance with liberal democracy, the social democratic indicators appear, rather clearly, to be moving in the negative direction. Social values of individuals as well as behavioural patterns of groups have degenerated in such a manner and to such an extent that they are threatening to destroy the overarching value of liberal democracy. What is most striking about the process of democratic social transformation is that, in the five decades of Indian Republic, more and more caste groups are sliding towards backwardness. If there were fewer Backward Castes during the year 1950, today that number has risen, with many more claims awaiting "degradation". Why is such a 'degradation' taking place in an ever increasing manner? As democracy is almost reduced to a game of numbers, the political process has found a vested interest in the segregation, rather than 'consolidation' and integration of all the people as citizens. Political parties are out-bidding each other in the pursuit of power, in the full knowledge that they are perpetrating by creating vested interests in the 'backwardness' instead of solving the problems of backwardness so as to move towards a state of full integration and equal citizenship.

A bizarre reflection of the contemporary political process is that the National Integration Committee was set up as a 'think-tank' of seven statesmen. It has grown into a massive National Integration Council (NIC) providing membership to about 400 people representing various 'interests' and 'identities'. That the composition, sise and character of the NIC today reflects a gross distortion is confirmed by the "thinking" process of its members, who demanded that the Ram *Mandir* versus Babri Masjid dispute locked up in the Judicial system, be referred to the NIC for a resolution. This grotesque thinking is by no means confined to the so called social institutions but has spread into the institutions of state through the route of "competitive populism" in its virulent form. One of the manifestations of this phenomenon is that – only women are appointed to the National Women's Commission; so is the case with Minorities Commission, SC & ST Commission, *et al*, both at the national and state levels, with the consequence that instead of facilitating harmonisation and integration they tend to accentuate the pre-existing conditions of social discord and emotional distress. As conflict has become the mode, officially sanctified over a period of time, more and more demands are made for ever more segregated commissions. It is a design and a process suited for social discord and for national disintegration. When Christians fight for their rights, and seek protection of their interests through a commission exclusively of Christian members, and so is the case with Muslims, Backward Castes, Scheduled Tribes, Women, Children, linguistic minority groups, economically backward sections – what emerges is an aggregation of a majority of minorities, with a minority left to search for the citizens of the nation. This process represents a regression of constitutionlal democracy.

This bizarre model of nation-building is the result of the formation of political parties and pursuit of power on the basis of the fragmented identities in turn prompting and perpetuating such fractured identities among the people. This is all the consequence of the distorted 'power process' indulged in by "pygmies" – a process that has ejected all traces of statesmanship. May be the vision set by the Constitution – we the people – is beyond the comprehension of the present day leadership. It is in this context, a second vision suggested by President APJ Abdul Kalam acquires a strategic significance for initiating the process of building a base for the development of India as a nation.

Wealth generation as a basis of socio-economic development can be accelerated through a recognition of the need for value-addition which is a function of integration of productivity in agriculture, bio-diversity and technology[12]. Inorder to derive the advantage of convergence and synergy, India has to graduate to a position where both bio-diversity and technology are in their prime. This will lead to value addition in agriculture. Such a mission can be accomplished only by promoting complementarity of roles between the politicians, administrators, technocrats and extension workers with a unified vision. This developmental model and process alone can possibly convert the conflict-mode into a collaborative mode of development and shared values of citizenship and nationalism. True democratic mode promotes and integrates development and harmony, inseparably.

The present situation is one where no one can win, it is too fragmented. So there is no threat to the integrity of the nation. But what is emerging from this existing disorder is a condition similar to a civil war, where all the fragmented groups' fight among themselves, but no one knows against whom? The conditions are conducive to anarchy. The existing Constitutional order may break-down, but how can an alternate vision emerge out of a pulverised society? Is there an alternative vision to fight for? The situation squarely meets the adage "chopping the branch on which one is perched". When so many groups are perched on the different branches, the tree may get destroyed. We need statesmen to renew and revive the constitutional democracy of India, promoting a fusion of skills, and motivation for socio-legal engineering.

As the state is engaged in the task of protecting the people, especially the weak against the strong, people's organisations (NGOs) picked up momentum in the sphere of socio-legal engineering. However, in place of partnership and participation peoples' organisations and the Indian state are pitted against each other, in a confrontationist disposition – massing in the form of PIL – where mostly it was the people who won against the state in the judicial portals. On occasions, the distortions of socio-economic development have led to movements with ascribed labels such as 'left-wing extremism'. Such situations when remained unresolved for long spells of time, acquire a place on the larger canvas of human rights and civil liberties.

Organised concern for human rights in India emerged when the civil liberties union was formed in 1936, aimed at fighting the violations by the British Rulers. The concerns were crystallised and incorporated in the Constitution as a part of democratic agenda, and Rule of Law. However, the positive efforts made to translate the concerns into a reality were found to be neither matching, nor adequate with the consequence that there was a discernible slide in human rights, especially in regard to those such as Scheduled Tribes who needed the protection most.

The distortions of the democratic process have impeded the emergence and consolidation of nationalism in India. These distortions, interrelated as they are, can be categorised variously. In essence they are : (a) the electoral process as the basic democratic process of the pursuit of power is abused, fragmenting the people into a large majority of religious, regional, linguistic, ethnic and caste minorities leading to a regression of the spirit of nationalism, and even worse, the emergence of regional and other minority parties, (b) statutorily supported 'reservations' to religious minorities and backward, scheduled castes and tribes. These impediments to nation-building and national integrity are sought to be legitimised and internalised through unofficial, but openly fought for 'reservations' to the diverse numerical groups leading to (c) an all pervasive, confrontationist culture in the polity as much as between the citizens and the state. While democracy offered the hope of progression and inclusivism, fundamentalism in Indian democracy generated the rage of intolerance, exclusivism, and regression. Lions kill to eat, foxes start biting off flesh from the body of their prey, even before killing.

The proceedings of the Constituent Assembly best represented the process of consensus across the political (and ideological) spectrum. The process was characterised by consent of the minority and not by a vote of the majority. That was how the vision of India, including its democratic governance was chiselled. However, very soon, during the early decades of democracy, even before the democratic consensualism was internalised and institutionalised, the democratic ethic got mauled in many ways. The political process, which renews, or could distort and destroy democracy, was vitiated by the basic process of power. Partisan pursuit of power vitiated socio-legal engineering of the Indian polity.

4.4. Progression – Regression

A country of continental character, carrying a backlog of challenges would take decades, if not centuries to catch-up with the past and move forward on the democratic path of progress. Five decades merely provide a milestone, not the end of the journey, certainly not the dead-end. A nation in the making can only pause, look-back and derive satisfaction that it is on course, not off the track. Such a pause also affords an opportunity to make mid-course corrections if any. There are several parameters that would help such an appraisal, within the framework of constitutional democracy, good governance and social transformation. Here, it is intended to take a satellite view of the nation on the move, and the progressive and regressive trends that emerged during the first five decades.

It was Plato who gave us the idea of a preamble. Every law must be preceded by a preamble, explaining the goal, as otherwise piling of interpretations or misinterpretations lead to distortion of the objectives of any specific legislation. Our experience of 50 years reveals that the preamble has not saved our Constitution from being diverted and perverted. Even more, the preamble itself was altered by the Parliament. And, such an 'alteration' was held by the judiciary as an unalterable "basic structural" feature. There is no clarification as to how concepts that were not there *ab initio,* at the starting point, but were incorporated at a later point of time could become "basic" and unalterable. The Judiciary also held that the basic structural features will be open for judicial scrutiny which also means subject to change by the judiciary. A process of change over a period may also mean and lead to a 'transplant'. Thus, the interpolations and interpretations of the Preamble have blurred and could continue to cloud the vision of the Constitution of India.

The legislature had not only incorporated hazy, dogmatised "concepts" of 'secularism' and 'socialism' into the preamble but also failed in translating such embedded directives, the "content" of these tenets. The legislatures also endorsed the proposition of the judiciary that the Directive Principles, the soul of the Constitution, are not justiciable. The judiciary got glued to the postulate of 'non-justifiability' and rejected the citizens' plea that public policy cannot go against the spirit of the Directive Principles. Thus, the centrality of constitutional 'soul' and the 'vision' have been reduced to a debate over labels; the substance has been lost sight of, causing incalculable damage to the Republic during the take-off decades.

Instead of compliance with the explicit and clear Directives, the institutions of the state have let loose an acrimonious debate, emerging from the labels of 'socialism' and 'secularism', leading to an enormous and growing volume of social strife. We remain in the debating and declaratory phase and have not yet entered the phase of clarity of the vision, and conviction and commitment towards its translation.

A constitution represents a statement of intent and facilitates the process of social transformation. Just as the survival of a high yielding variety of seed depends upon factors such as the quality of soil, water management and climatic conditions, the efficacy of even the most ideal constitution depends upon the social conditions, the institutions and processes of governance the critical variable being the leadership of a country. Our founding fathers observed unanimously, as of 1990s, that the Constitution has stood the test of time. They thought that it is not the Constitution that is at fault for some of the unhappy things that took place. The fault is laid at the doors of those who implemented, and in the process circumvented it.[13]

One can derive a great deal of satisfaction that the people and the leaders have not rejected the Constitution as it happened in many of the countries in the developing world. But one thing that cannot be denied is that while the trappings of 'constitutionalism' are maintained, there has been a steady decline in the 'culture' that sustains the Constitution, any constitution.

Members of the Consembly were confident that the country is large and mightier than the transitional problems that it would be facing during the early decades. People, they felt, would become more and more conscious and that out of all these dark forces the angel of hope would arise. There are certainly 'many miles to go' and the nation has the strength and determination to fulfil its aspirations and hopes. In the end it is the enlightened citizens who constitute the best instrumentality of a constitution-not only in effectuating it, but also in exercising a check on its abuse.

The founding fathers laid great hope, ultimately, in the development of democratic conventions in place of recurring constitutional amendments. It was generally accepted and acknowledged by the Consembly that the Constitution cannot remain static and rigid. In the light of experience derived from (a) the working of our Constitution, (b) the numerous amendments effected, (c) the concept of 'basic structure' enunciated (though not defined) by the Supreme Court, and, (d) the emerging power-equations and points of friction between the trinity of instrumentalities of state, our Constitution needs a holistic review, and fine-tuning, not dramatic, much less traumatic, change.

As Justice Brandies of the U.S. Supreme Court once said of the American Constitution, it is not a straight jacket. It is a living organism. As such it is capable of growth or expansion and of adaptation to new conditions. Indians have grown conscious of the liberal institutions of the legislature, the executive's responsibility to the legislature, judicial supremacy in matters of interpretation, the theory of separation of powers and checks and balances in the Constitution. It would be incorrect to say that these institutions have not taken root in India. The credit for retaining and stabilising our democracy goes to the *demos*, the citizens at large. Guy Soran has observed, from an entirely different angle, "in fifty years, India did much to build the state, it did little to build the people of India. Indian state has grown into a mighty banyan tree, but it has not contributed to good governance".[14]

The largest written Constitution with 395 Articles and 12 Schedules, reflected the concern and anxiety of the Founding Fathers to offer constitutional methods and solutions to many of the socio-economic problems of the country. Democratisation meant a movement from a situation of 'continuum' towards 'convergence'. The convergence blue-print envisioned integration of democratic mode as the process, with development as the substance, both reinforcing each other, through good governance.

The constitutional concerns continue to be echoed, with resonance, by some leaders of the day. Modern man intensely needs the vision of life if the achievements of science and technology are not to lead him to greater and greater destruction - but sublimation in achieving majestic heights of creative living. The vision of India, *Sampoorna Swaraj,* has been reflected as encompassing a large spectrum of humanist ideals. Some of the reflections of the wise among the observers also reveal perceived shortfalls during the first five decades. H.H. Swamy Chidanand Saraswatiji observes that Indian culture is a treasure chest of wisdom, insight and universal truths which can cure the afflictions of war, violence and despair plaguing the world today. Mother India's place in the world should be, he adds, one of a great leader, a moral guide, a torch-bearer of peace, piety, devotion, trend-setter and path-finder. Swami Jayendra Saraswati, the Sankaracharya of Kanchi Mutt calls for regaining India's lost direction for a better future for the present generation and for posterity. The commitment on the part of a *Bharateeya* to pursue a life conforming to *Dharma* makes him or her bound to doing duties more than demanding rights. Swamy Ranganadhananda laments that free India is far away. A common identity of Indianness, sense of pride, equality, caring–sharing are some of the vital requisites for building a nation. They are yet to be infused into the national-life stream.[15]

There are priorities and prerequisites of democratic development ranging from health-care, education, shelter and salvation from starvation, to a transparent political system and a highly disciplined government. President A.P.J. Abdul Kalam extols the need for commitment to spiritual socialism, respecting the freedom of others, and the need to protect, nurture and build on development so that India moves rapidly towards a self-reliant and self-assured development nation, gaining military and economic strength to be able to stand up to the world. In this perspective, A.P.J. Abdul Kalam focussed on the need for a "second vision aimed at alleviating poverty, illiteracy and unemployment to place India in the category of developed nations . . . ". In his address to the nation on the eve of the 55th anniversary of Independence A.P.J. Abdul Kalam, the President of India underlined that : non-violence, tolerance and acceptance of all religions and the fearless search for truth were values taught by the Mahatma, and they were the "corner-stones of our civilisational heritage" and therefore of the Indian polity. It was this "pluralistic tradition" and the civilisational heritage of thousands of years over which a "unique fusion" of multiple cultures, religions and ways of life had taken place. Pinpointing the role of leadership as a live dynamic force, A.P.J. Abdul Kalam observed that the youth needed role models from the present generation, not just from the past when the freedom movement threw up a galaxy of tall men. Members of Parliament and legislatures could shape the future of children by becoming role-models. "Parliament and legislatures have a crucial role in shaping the vision of developed India and value-based polity".[16]

The vision of the Constitution of India truly represents universality – which can be translated into reality. It is not merely good governance, but a leadership of all sectors of the nation to adopt a mission mode. The Constitution of India is not just a chronicle of Articles, but represents one Article of Faith.

References

1. B.R. Ambedkar. The Constitution and Constituent Assembly, Salient Features of the Constitution. Reply to the Debate No. 25, 1949 p. 177.
2. Mahatma Gandhi, Hindusthan Times, New Delhi, 28 Jan. 1948.
3. Mahatma Gandhi.
4. Jawaharlal Nehru, The Constitution and Constituent Assembly, Salient Features of the Constitution, p. 56.
5. M.S. Swaminathan, Indicators of Human Development. The Hindu, Hyderabad, Sunday 25 Nov. 2002 p. I and Sunday Apr. 7, 2003.
6. George Monbiet The Hindu Jan 29, 2004, Hyderabad p. 5.
7. Gupta SP. "Trickle Down Theory Revisited : The role of employment and poverty" VB Singh Memorial Lecture, New Delhi 1999.
8. B.R. Ambedkar in his final intervention, 25 Nov. 1949. The Constituent Assembly and the Constitution.
9. Judith R. Masers (ed) Roussean Jean Jaques : On Social Contract. New York, A Martin's Press 1978.
10. Keith Griffin in Dean Baker et al (eds) Globalizaiton and Progressive Economic Policy. Cambridge, Cambridge University Press 1998 p. 94.
11. G.R.S. Rao, Delivery of Social Justice to the Tribal communities; Social Justice under the Constitution of India; Journal of APJA, Hyderabad 1992.
12. For a detailed consideration, refer APJ Abdul Kalam (with A Sivathanu Pillay) Envisioning an Empowered Nation, Tata McGraw Hill, New Delhi '2004.

13. GRS Rao, Constitution of India, Vision, Reality and Reform, Centre for Public Policy and Social Development, Hyderabad 1998.
14. Guy Soran.
15. Vision of India Bhavan's Journal Bharatiya Vidya Bhavan, Bombay Jan. 2003.
16. Abdul Kalam APJ Independence Day eve address to the Nation (14 Aug. 2002). The Hindu, Hyderabad Aug. 15 2002 p. 1.

5

CONSTITUTIONAL DEFICIT

An Appraisal

There has been quite a sporadic as well as protracted public debate on the working of the Constitution, on the need for a review and reform, and some voice in favour of a second Constituent Assembly inorder to frame a second constitution, *de novo*. The debate *per se* suggests that the Republic is vibrant. Public discourse on 'reform' and 'rewriting' is conducted within the framework of 'constitutionalism'. Time may not be running out for such as corrective measures a thorough review and of the Constitution, apart from promoting an enabling environment within which the Constitution functions to its full potential. However, there are quite a few forces and groups on the fringe, which constitute a threat to the spirit of constitutionalism. The adage that eternal vigil is the price of democracy is even more relevant in relation to the environment within which the Constitution is working. This is so because of the anti-democratic forces operating both within and outside the country. As the borders between nations are melting, thanks to the factors such as globalisation, liberalisation, information and communication science and technology, threats to national security and integrity can now be programmed by an alliance between the external forces and internal sources of discord.

Social strife and destabilisation provide the potential ground conditions for constitutional stress, strain and breakdown. Hence the critical significance of an appraisal and course-correction where found necessary. Such an appraisal, a diagnosis, confirms the fears that it is a 'virus' that has infected and afflicted India's constitutional democracy. When a virus is left unattended, or wrongly diagnosed and treatment attempted, the Constitution itself could get debilitated. It is this virus rather than any inherent deficiency that is severely affecting the working of the Constitution. The constitutional 'deficit' in the Indian polity is induced critically by the virus within the polity. An appraisal of the 'constitutional deficit' in India reveals five sets of interrelated factors: They are (a) Distortions of the Vision, (b) Faulted processes of 'power'; (c) Managerial Deficit in Governance, (d) Impaired umpiring of the working of the Constitution, and, (e) the backlash of the process of according primacy to the letter of the Constitution over the spirit of constitutionalism. None of these factors is inherent within the Constitution, but emanate from the environment within which the Constitution is operating. This deficit is discussed here illustratively, but not exhaustively.

5.1. Distortions of The Vision

The constitutional vision (a) represents the best features of liberal democracy, (b) sets its sights far ahead of its times beyond what could be seen with a naked eye, and (c) it is validated by the legitimacy, integrity and credibility of the early leaders being 'truly' representive of the people. It can also be stated that the vision is also reinforced and validated by five decades of constitutional democracy in India. The most significant aspect of carving out the vision of India was that it was formulated through a consensual process, by statesman who were inspired by the Indian civilisation and participated in the mainstream of freedom movement. They had the courage of conviction, above the partisan, and did not have any partisan political axe to grind.

A preamble cannot be 'amended', by a partisan vote, without a mandate. It can be chiselled, perhaps for clarity through a process of consensus, but not nibbled. The latter-day incorporation of 'socialism' and 'secularism' into the preamble has blurred the vision, dogmatised the ideals of liberal democracy, and polarised the nation into a majority and minorities, and the 'haves' and 'have-nots'. The collapse of socialism as well as capitalism during the closing years of 20th century demonstrated that dogma cannot stand the test of time. A short-sighted partisan process packed such a dogma into the preamble causing the greatest damage to the vision and mission of India. The legislation enacted by the parliament on Muslim Women's Right to Property, and the Supreme Court's verdict on the legislation, and several such instances reveal how the vision of the Constitution was distorted, by the partisan political process.

The integrals of democracy viz. decentralisation of 'power', and equitable, participative development, representing the processual and the substantive dimensions of participative democracy have been distorted and mutilated equally. The ill-effects of such distortions almost negated the quality of democratic process. In spite of the constitutional amendments (73rd & 74th), India today is much more a highly centralised democracy than at the starting line.

Disparities have grown, people are being marginalised faster. India is growing prosperous but people are being empoverished. The tribal communities, for whose protection and welfare special provisions have been made in the Constitution would have been better off if they were left untouched by the process of development. The number of Scheduled Castes has risen from 10 in 1947 to more than 100 today. The number of Scheduled Tribes has grown from 6 in 1947 to more than 60 today. The challenge of managing the humanist vision of India was focussed on the twin tasks of (a) improving the human condition, and (b) promoting and sustaining harmonious human relations. The challenge of change was to convert the status of 'people' into 'citizens' exuding *espirit de crops* and national identity. The nature and quality of democratic governance and economic growth were the constitutional means to achieve this humanist vision and mission. But, right from the start, we had lost sight of this ends and means harmonisation. We aimed at reducing the regional imbalances and thus located major industrial and developmental projects in backward 'areas', and assumed that it will *ipso facto* contribute to the development and integration of the 'people' in the backward areas. In reality, we had witnessed, consistently throughout the first five decades, the unintended consequence of further degradation of the standards and quality of life of the local (and indigenous) populations. The migratory patterns had led to alienation and conflict in the form of 'locals' versus 'outsiders'. The locals whose backwardness was sought to be remedied most often ended up as 'migrants-in-distress'; or worse 'aliens' on their own lands. At a different level, industrial policy has been formulated as early as 1956, and upgraded continuously, with significant turning points. We have not formulated a cogent agricultural policy, but implemented momentary impulses, in shaping agriculture, ignoring the agricultural communities.

What is true of the vision is even more so with regard to the directions and directives envisioned by the Constitution. The partisan processes and standards were evident in more ways than one, in regard to these directions. Every political party, while in power, did precious little to act in tune with the Directive Principles, while all the parties when sitting in 'opposition' criticised those in government for not implementing the Directive Principles. Even while betraying their duplicity by legislating some provisions against the spirit of the Directive Principles, political parties had tried to justify their actions on grounds of 'non-justifiability'. On some occasions, the partisans had demonstrated duplicity by selectively and dramatically shifting some provisions of Directive Principles such as education and Panchayati Raj into Fundamental Rights, but without matching follow-up action.

Any argument that the vision set out at the very inception of the Constitution was deficient or distorted begs the question as to what could be those deficiencies. Any argument that the vision in its entirety is distorted similarly raises the question of an alternative vision that can be formulated, and different direction set for the nation. No organised public opinion or political party has either pin-pointed any deficiency or deformity in the vision, much less coherently articulated an alternative vision.

Any argument that the postulate of "basic structure" enunciated by the Supreme Court tends to freese the vision of the Constitution is not sustainable as the Court has kept the doors open for itself to add, delete or modify the basic structural features of the Constitution. Independent of the authority thus reserved for itself, the Constitution itself has provided for (a) a review and revision as well as (b) advisory referenceto the Judiciary. The evolutionary process was not sealed.

Those who constitute the fringe, who demand a second constituent assembly even without an idea of an alternative vision, do not recognise that such a proposal is riddled with a set of questions and issues, the resolution of which would be far more complex and difficult than the perceived problems underlying the argument for a second constitution. Some of these questions are : (a) what would be the composition of the second constituent assembly, (b) how such an assembly will be brought into existence? (c) how and on what alternatives of vision would the candidates or parties contest or claim for membership of such a consembly (d) would they adopt an alternative vision / concept by a majority, two-thirds or a simple), or through a consensual process (d) would they fuse the different alternative, if not conflicting visions, or accept one and reject the rest. The most critical of all the issues would be whether an alternative vision could protect the integrity and promote the unity of the nation, so as to be able to pursue that vision in unison. Such a unison is most unlikely because the issue itself represents, a 'political' agenda, not based on concerns for constitutionalism. A related basic question is what is it that the Parliament working under the present Constitution cannot shape? And if it cannot, how can it create a Consembly and empower it to do what it cannot by itself do?

Twentieth century had witnessed several countries adopting and experimenting divergent ideological forms of governance in their endeavour to promote nation-building. All of them had recognised that neither ideology nor the form of government *per se* could determine the process of development, in a manner as to lend stability and credibility to the structures of state as well as to the country. It was in this background of 20th century experiments with and experiences of governance and of democracy the world over, the vision of the Constitution of India stands vindicated. The debate on Directive Principles of State Policy cannot be confined to 'justiciability' they have to be activated, not as a political expediency, but as the vital force of democratic social transformation. The Directive Principles represent the core of liberal democratic ethic, the universal humanist vision and the mission of the Constitution of India.

5.2. Faulted Process of Power

The people of India vested their sovereign 'power' with their duly elected representatives as trustees inorder to enable them to perform a set of complementary roles and tasks for the promotion of a set of common objectives, in consonance with the spirit of liberal democracy. They recognised the role and place of the media and of the other institutions of civil society and assigned a distinctive set of complementary roles enabling all of them contribute towards the fulfilment of the mission of the Constitution. The political parties had been recognised as the 'prime movers', and entrusted with the overarching role of 'managing trustees' of this national, democratic, constitutional power-grid.

In the brief history of our Republic, too soon after winning political freedom, carving out our national vision, and commencing our long pilgrimage of nation-building, how come the people of India today seem to have become the victims at the hands of their own 'trustees', and the managing trustees? While the citizens are searching for answers and corrective measures, the 'actors' are engaged in the deflection of issues and mutual recrimination. There is a widespread loss of confidence in the leaders, but not in the constitutional democratic system. Even a cursory analysis clearly reveals that the process of power is faulted, with the result that the institutions of state have been enervated. When there are massive leakages, pilferages, line-losses, load distortions, fluctuating voltage, and breakdowns, they will have their detrimental impact on the democratic polity as a whole.

The situation in which the people of India find themselves in, is not the making of one day or of any one individual or any single institution. It has not been this bad from the starting line; if it were so, we would have gone through a phase of diverse manifestations or mutations of democracy, labelled as monarchic, guided, protected, controlled, centralised, partyless, presidential, parliamentary, militarised and marketised *et al.* The first five decades can be broadly delineated into three stages marking the gradual slide in the democratic standards of the 'elected' as well as the 'selected' managers, and in the functioning of the institutions of constitutional democracy. The three spells can be marked as (i) 1950–65, (ii) 1965–80, and (iii) 1981–2000, that have witnessed gradually and consistently fading standards of democracy.

The first phase proved to be fairly smooth as it was characterised by the same political party running governments both at the center and in the states, supported by relatively upright administration, both operating under the spill-over of the 'spirit' of freedom movement. There have been some minor aberrations. The second spell (1965-80) had witnessed stresses and strains where the political executive tended to take the legislature for granted, and attempted to condition the judiciary through suppression and imposing and infusing an ethos of extra-constitutional "commitment". The play of extra-constitutional forces became predominant in terms of centralisation of power, extensive use and abuse of Article 356, and most important of all, the proclamation of 'emergency' vitiated both by intent as well as the process. The third stage (1980 – 2000) was marked by politically ignited turbulence revolving round reservations policy; center-state and inter-state discord leading to antagonistic and hostile dispositions and discourse; and a contrived debate over issues such as secularism; and role-conflict between the institutions of state. The new and rapid spread of genes of corruption afflicting the institutional network as a whole, has emerged as a serious threat to constitutional democracy in India.

Dr. Ambedkar's words of concern for the smooth functioning of constitutional democracy in India are prophetic, for, he cautioned : "If we wish to maintain democracy not merely in form, but also in fact, what must we do? The first thing in my judgement, we must hold fast to constitutional methods of achieving our social and economic objectives. It means we must abandon the bloody methods of revolution. It means that we must abandon the method of civil disobedience, non cooperation and *Satyagraha*. When there was no way left for constitutional methods for achieving economic and social objectives, there was a great deal of justification for unconstitutional methods. But, where constitutional methods are open, there can be no justification for these unconstitutional methods. These methods are nothing but the methods of anarchy, and the sooner they are abandoned, the better for us".[1]

With the first democratic elections in 1951 the Indian National Congress assumed power both at the center as also in all the states. There was no recognised, or even a recognizable 'opposition', much less an 'alternative'. Ideologically, the entire spectrum was reflected within the Indian National

Congress (INC). Over a period of time, there emerged a multitude of political parties – some based on fragmented ideology, many more due to 'personality' factors better expressed as cult. Some parties emerged with 'regional' agenda. The picture could be summed up as one of power-oriented fragmentation rather than ideological or programatic polarisation. In a manner, all the parties had committed to the constitutional agenda, mixed economy, 'secular' ethos, eradication of caste, provision of basic human needs, and the like. That there was no strong ideological variance was confirmed even as late as in 1991, when the INC initiated liberalisation was accepted by all the parties, including the left oriented, and all states. Then how can any one explain the emergence of as many as 621 parties registered with the Election Commission including 8 national and 39 state level 'recognised' parties, as of the year 2000? During the era of coalition governments (1970 to 2000) literally every 'party' joined hands with every other party, in at some state, and some-time or the other. There emerged also the phenomena of (a) opposing a given party at the state level and supporting the same party at the centre, and (b) extending support from 'outside'; without sharing the responsibility for the wrong-doings of the party so supported. Even more significant is the phenomenon of those parties who fought elections bitterly opposing each other, joining hands soon after elections to form coalitions. This political process has grown into an Indian version of a grand alliance of the evil.

'Abstention' from voting in the national as well as state legislatures, and 'whipping' the participation and voting as per 'party-line' within the legislatures has contributed, in no small measure, to the debasement of democratic process, and of the legislatures. Such practices have also led to a power-shift from the people and their representatives to the political party 'High-command'. Indian democracy emerged as a mutation of 'command democracy'. Even one-man party was no exception to this phenomenon. Today any discourse of any or many issues such as; (a) leadership; (b) internal democracy (c) emergence, of a 'party', constitution and enrolment of membership (d) democratic character, (e) sources of funds, and accountability for expenditure, and most important (f) modes of acquisition, exercise and retention of power, (g) ideological and programmatic agenda, if any, and (h) accountable performance in tune with their respective manifesto and public mandate. In the end, the 'sovereign' citizens are edged out of the democratic process. Every facet of party system and its management can be summed up as "corporatisation" of political power, operating outside the framework of constitutional and statutory provisions. If this absence of constitutional or statutory status and accountability cannot be described as "law-lessness", the situation may have to be summed up as 'above-the-law', but certainly not within the normative framework of any law.

Authoritarian leadership with the euphemism of 'high command', unrelated to grass-root base, and ruthless bidding for power with competitive – populism, have criminalised the political process. Their crimes employ all the means of money and muscle power, contrived social conflicts based on caste, region, language and sharing of natural resource such as water. None of the means is excluded in achieving their end objective of capturing power. During the early decades they could secure power by purchasing votes, and free flow of liquor; they graduated thereafter to capturing the ballot boxes and polling booths; now instead of going through that 'rig-morale', they prefer to buy elected representatives in the bulk, in a no-holds-barred situation to capture and retain power. Peoples' representatives are commandeered, highjacked and physically confined; in cattle-sheds earlier, and in five-star hotels now. Today the process is 'elevated' and turned into a more sophisticated mode in tune with 'liberalisation'. Today, political parties are operated by leaders with the finess of Chief Executive Officers of corporate organisations; whose prime focus is on investments, mergers, joint ventures, buy-backs, insider-trading and all the corporate trappings of a market economy. Indian democracy is marketised.

The Indian political functionaries, like the pick-pockets, try to deflect the attention of the public (towards the moon), pick the pockets of gullible people and disappear. The politicians make all the promises that they know they cannot fulfil in five years. They are in the full knowledge that their performance has no correlation to their promises. And their actions have no relationship to what they project in the manifesto, copies of which are not available even in the party offices. Most of the promises remain unfulfilled, and most of their major actions are not in confirmity with their manifestos. Their actions are impulsive, designed to retain power, at any cost, and to retain it at all costs.

The essentially secular polity is irreparably fractured due to communal 'vote' politics. The manner in which all the political parties state that the "era of coalition governments has come to stay", sounds like the Republic is converted into a joint-stock company. Representatives who are elected on the basis of fragmented identities and vote-banks fail to recognise that they have to represent the total population of 'their' constituency. They continue to represent their caste, community, region and party even as members of the national Parliament. As the Legislatures exhibit loss of primacy, and gets on to the streets, the people are left to debate the 'problems' of the Legislatures.

Two fundamental distortions have been brought into play in regard to the character of *Rajya Sabha* viz., (a) annulling the residential requirement, and (b) switch over to open ballot from secret ballot, both are prompted by partisan political process, and in violation of the character of the *Rajya Sabha* as the council of states.

When the Chief Election Commissioner brought out a list of as many as 20 Members elected to the *Rajya Sabha* who did not meet the legislated "residential" norm, instead of protecting the norm as a constitutional convention the Parliament simply negated the norm. And this inspite of the norm highlighted by Dr. Ambedkar that the Rajya Sabha represented the states, and Sarkaria Commission's observation that the *Rajya Sabha* would be more federal when several states are not ruled by the same party as the one in power at the centre. It is a clear case of partisan political interests taking precedence over democratic norms and constitutional conventions.

That the basic process of power is distorted, decimating the democratic character of the polity, is reflected in the frequency of appointment of commissions and committees meant to reform the political system. The output of wisdom flowing from these commissions and committees on electoral reforms was matched only by total inaction. There are only three issues that transcend the frosen dispositions of 'ruling' versus 'opposition' politics. These three are; (a) deadly inaction on reforming the power process through electoral reforms, (b) consensual silence over regular increases in remuneration, and allowances as well as perks and facilities, and (c) constantly 'add on' privileges absolutely unrelated to their performance as legislators. At the end of more than 20 reports of commissions and committees on electoral reforms, the only consensual measure hurriedly formulated (but could not be rushed through the Parliament) was the one on state funding of elections. Containing the costs of elections that have become untenable by democratic norms and Indian standards has been ejected consensually. All this could happen because the power process has been so hijacked that the demos have become captives. In sheer democratic terms, this situation can be described as 'contempt of citizens'.

The political process, which is the prime mover of a democratic polity, has shifted its focus from the articulation of public issues, harmonisation of competing values and conflicting interests, and forging of common Indian national identity. The present process distortions have diluted the differentiation between the different political parties on the one hand, and also as between the party, the government, and the state on the other. The political malignancy is spreading to the whole body politic. The representative character of the elected functionaries is so severely jolted that today an individual without black money, muscle power, and some degree of kinship (which includes extended mutations of caste, sub-caste, and religious identity), cannot contest democratic elections. The 'feudal' order of the past is resurrected with vengeance, in the form of political power structures and styles. A senior statesman once observed that a candidate's defeat in the elections in contemporary times (1990s) is a vindication of his honesty and character. Conversely success in elections represents conclusive proof of dishonesty.

Political morality, and schooling for democracy (from entry level *Panchayat* bodies and graduation to state level-legislatures ultimately leading to

Parliament), witnessed during the early stages of democratisation has given way to a revival of political feudalism, and corporate ethos of investment, (most political party leaders selling party-tickets to the competitive bidders), and 'returns' in forms such as quotas for telephones, gas cylinders to outlets, industrial licences, engineering and medical colleges; all such 'returns' ultimately expanding in range to cover protection to the criminals who would have been awarded, if and when prosecuted, life sentence and death penalty. Almost all the political parties started arguing on the lines of survival in an atmosphere of competitive bidding among the parties.

Where the political process and the institutions as the prime-movers get so afflicted due to the faulted processes of power, it is only logical that the complementary institutions get exposed to the virus of the polluted political stream. First it was the executive institutions that gradually converted their complementarity into collusion and nexus, with the judiciary not saved from this expanding visçious environment. All the institutions of state – the legislative, executive and judicial on the horizontal plane; and the union, state and local tiers on the vertical plane got afflicted by this faulted process of 'power'; their respective roles and common constitutional objectives were distorted. The soil conditions became fertile, not for democracy but, for the myriad forms of corruption, to grow and flourish. Democratic process is corrupted by the virus of political malignancy.

On the vertical plane the centre resorted to dismissal of state governments, on no less than 110 times, under Article 356. An Emergency was imposed on the country as a whole, purely on personal and political partisan grounds. The centre had despatched central police, paramilitary as well as armed forces to the states at their own request, as well as at its own suggestion on grounds of internal as well as border security management, nearly on a thousand times. Yet, Article 355 had not been invoked on a technical plea that the central forces can go to the assistance of any part of a state only on receipt of a request from the District Magistrate concerned.

Even in the face of massive mal administration and pending cases of misappropriation on the part of state governments, they did not hesitate issuance of public threats in advance to the constitutional units of *Panchayat Raj* that they would be stripped of their powers if they failed to provide relief to the drought affected mandals. It is not only the institutions of *Panchayati Raj*, but also statutory cooperative institutions that were used and abused as the instruments of political power. Members of Parliament Local Area Development Scheme (MPLADS), and its copy cat Members of State Legislatures Scheme represent an unabashed encroachment on *Panchayati Raj* institutions and functionaries and also a dilution if not destruction of their respective roles. It is a fit case for a PIL petition. Democratic ethic, process and institutions are corrupted by the virus of political malignancy.

The appointments of so called Judicial / Quasi-Judicial Commissions in India makes a farce of the constitutional provisions. Some details of such commissions reflect a pattern. A state commission with a retired Judge as Chair and three others as members for Backward Classes came into existence during 1994 on the basis of a state legislation enacted in the wake of an agitation. After the expiry of one term of three years, it was given an extension of a second term, followed by six-month extension each for five times. In reality, it took eight and a half years but could not formulate any concrete recommendations. Neither the Commission sought, nor the Government gave any further extension. In the given situation if and when a new panel is appointed, it may start the work *de novo* rather than start where the earlier commission left. At what cost, no functionary seems responsible and accountable. The fact that as many as 109 new claims have been made seeking BC status to the existing number of 92 reveals that problems keep growing, institutions get proliferated but without resolution of the problems. Indian scenario affords an apt reality to study the phenomenon of 'sleeping commissions' which serve partisan political expediency, deflection of issues, and in keeping members of the judiciary "busy". India also affords rich data to examine, jurisprudentially, as to how and what differentiates 'sitting' or 'retired' members of the judiciary when appointed to any 'Judicial Commission of inquiry'. The individual, his status (retired or sitting), and the method that makes it "Judicial" have been mixed up, and coloured. That is why and how, the demos are confused if not lost confidence in the judicial institutions and processes. Whether it is a case of political parties using, misusing and abusing the Judicial system, or the Judicial leadership allowing such misuse and abuse, the consequence is an image loss of the judicial institutions, leading to a 'loss of confidence'.

The Constitution and constitutional culture get reduced to a ball-game when a constitutional functionary of the status of Central Vigilance Commissioner commends the Public Interest Litigation route in fighting systemic corruption. Indian democracy has been a witness to a plethora of statutory regulatory institutions (insurance, telecommunications, electricity, *et al*). But, as the structures and procedures, as well as the mind-sets of these regulators are rooted in bureaucracy, these regulators are found, resenting rather than rejecting 'interference' from the governments. This institutional proliferation also has led to, with increasing frequency, to Jurisdictional conflict, loading the dockets in the Supreme Court and the High Courts. All these inter-institutional conflicts – horizontal, vertical and diagonal-pale into insignificance when compared to role-relationships of the two constitutional majors viz. the legislature and the judiciary. This conflict is growing in volume, frequency and intensity.

The citizens are excluded from the arena and confined to the grand-stand as spectators, witness to, and victims of the game of faulted process of power. The citizens have been watching and waiting for the rules of the game to be settled so that the state can attend to the constitutional role responsibilities of good governance, and the agenda of social transformation. They waited for the Constitutional Review Commission (NCRWC), hoped that it might focus on the citizen; it has come and gone as another instance of 'Commissions' allowing themselves sucked away by the political malignancies. It is in this background the citizens feel that there ought to develop a 'contempt of citizens' jurisprudence.

The President of India, A.P.J. Abdul Kalam touched the pulse of the citizens when he observed that "conduct and behaviour in public life are, like never before, under very close scrutiny". He emphasised "it was essential that the three pillars of democracy – Legislature, Judiciary and the Executive are strong in structure, pure in form and uncorrupted and unblemished in conduct". The first citizen made it clear that, "if we cannot make India corruption-free, then the vision of making the nation developed by 2020 would remain a dream". In this context, the members of the Judiciary "become inviolable role models, the perfect incorruptible ideals of civilised society" [2].

C. Rajagopalachari's statement that "we must rebuild our lost aristocracy, not of birth, not of wealth or even of intellect, but of character" emerges to be a critical requirement of our nation today than ever before. Issues of credibility and accountability are significantly influenced by the nature and quality of leadership – not only political, but also the leadership of various sectors of the society – religion, education, industry, and other professions. Indian society as a whole has suffered a decline in creative intellectualism and social leadership as much as, from the partisan political process. The credibility and efficacy of political leadership suffers from inadequate commitment to the constitutional values, obsessive concern for privileges, and a low appreciation of the fact that India is a country of masses who have to be delivered from the clutches of poverty and prejudices. The leadership of other sectors is devoid of a measure of professional ethics and accountability. An ethical base and a spiritual temper which characterised the freedom movement are found diminishing to the point of extinction in the Republic of India today. "Back in 1947, you could distinguish between 'bandits' and 'politicians', not now. That is a measure of how far we have fallen" lamented Achyut Patwardhan an illustrious leader of the freedom movement. A renewal of leadership thus has to start from ethical and spiritual premises, not mere electoral promises or process. The line of argument that "as a part of the society, our profession also suffers from the same evils" is not tenable, and not available to the creative leaders who have a responsibility to save, and shape the society.

5.3. Management and Governance

Guy Soran's observation warrants reinteraction : "in fifty years, India did much to build the state, it did little to build the people of India. Indian state has grown into a mighty banyan tree, but, it has not contributed to good governance" [3]. Indian experience validates the hypothesis that there is an inverse correlation between sise and productivity. The proliferation and expansion of the institutions of state have only contributed to the phenomenon of exclusion of citizens from participatory role, as much as irresponsive and irresponsible nature of administrative disposition towards citizens.

A more fundamental problem of management in governance in India is that in fifty years, it has not shed off its colonial dispositions of the alien rulers and times. The vacuum created by the Empire withdrawing from India is more than filled up by the empire-building, shared and thus reinforced equally by the elected and the appointed executives alike. As between the two, the initial friction caused by the transition towards democracy has been adjusted in terms of four-fold mutual dispositions viz. (a) positive cooptation, (b) withdrawal, (c) hostility, and (d) collusion and collaborative exploitation.

Licence-permit Raj may have vanished but red-tape and corruption have assumed virulent forms and expansive ethos. In their search for the "windows" of administration, citizens have grown frustrated and hostile towards the first court of Justice, that prompts them to move the Judicial courts of Justice where again there is a staggering volume of pending litigation. The waiting time spans two-three generations. The oft cited solution, as seen by the managers of government, is an increase in the numbers, a ratio in proportion to the growth rate in population. This reveals a status-quo mind set, closed to innovation, productivity and creativity. There is a preference in the administration to deal with cases individually, even if they are identical and thus amenable to resolution through changes in the systems and procedures. But where information is treated as power, and every individual case a source of extra money, reform is anathama. A strange phenomenon of management in government in India is that public servants do not perceive themselves as citizens in the first place; retirement from service is dreaded for they have to learn to live like a "common citizen". Judicialisation of issues of management at the political and administrative levels skews not only the process of governance, but equally the *inter-se* role relations between the various units and tiers of administration. The resultant friction could stall the entire machinery of government, people tend to resort to taking law into their hands which is nothing but lawlessness. The meek and the hapless, like the farmers, commit suicides. When the management process itself acquires the character of a disaster, it will, for sure, devastate democracy.

Information and Communication Technologies (ICT) can prove very effective in enhancing the managerial process in government. But ICT could be a good servant, or a bad master, depending upon the attitudinal dispositions and value system of the managers. There are clear indications that ICT, to the extent it is set in place, is being used to centralise rather than decentralise.

The call by statesmen leaders for adequate and appropriate knowledge management in governance as a means to empower the people, can unleash their potential in accelerating development and promotion of the quality of life.

5.4. Impaired Umpiring

As a consequence of the loss of credibility of the political process, the credibility of constitutional democracy in India is at stake. Due to the friction, the instrumentalities of state are heating up, stalling the march of the nation, and its constitutional agenda. Governance itself is faulted. In such a situation, how can the inadequacies in the working of the Constitution be analysed or explained without a reference to the wide range of functionaries who have been assigned, by the Constitution itself, the task of protecting and defending the Constitution? The architects of the Constitution conceived and sculpted a number of positions such as the President, the Governors, the Speakers of legislatures, the Supreme Court, the Election Commission and the like, and assigned them the task of umpiring the game of constitutional democracy in India. These institutions have been assigned 'autonomous' constitutional status so as to enable them to perform their role without fear or favour. The President, by virtue of his status, mode of election and oath of office stands out as the constitutional conscience-keeper, and the fountainhead of democratic governance.

The sacred task to "preserve, protect and defend the Constitution" came to the fore when Dr. Rajendra Prasad was the President and Jawaharlal Nehru the Prime Minister. The issue came up during the early stages, and was unfortunately projected and debated as one of "power" rather than as the 'role' of the President . Dr. Rajendra Prasad had seen the issue as a part of his 'role' as the constitutional conscience keeper, while Nehru had perceived and projected the issue in terms of 'power'. Role is complementary, power is unitary and hierarchical. But, the ego of Nehru had the day. As 'power' generates ego, the egoistic position was frosen in the form of an amendment to the Constitution rather than allowing the issue to crystalise as a 'convention'. Since then, the 'role' of President has been cast and almost accepted within the frosen mould of 'power'.

Distortions of 'power-play' in the interface management is straining, in an ever increasing manner, the image and role efficacy of the umpires. The constitutional umpires cannot always browse through the letter (Articles) for solutions to constitutional issues, missing or ignoring the 'spirit' of the Constitution, embedded in the debates in the Consembly constitutional conventions, democratic ethic and political morality.

Inorder to regain and sustain the efficacy of umpiring, and their own institutional image, the umpires should themselves set standards. Speakers of legislatures participating in political party conventions, and maneuvering ministerial berths; governors switching back and forth for electoral politics and ministerial berths; Chief Justices and Judges as Chairpersons and members of a variety of Commissions, (working towards securing other offices, national or international, while in office), all such practices lead to mix-up of roles. They constitute the 'contra-indicators' of the image and efficacy of umpiring, and the spirit of the Constitution. If the various political parties, though at different points of time, depending upon their absence or presence in the government, either at the centre or in the states, had accused that the office of Governors are being abused or misused, as the agents of the Centre, it is not only the political parties who have to explain the phenomenon collectively, but the persons, who held the august office, who have to explain. Can there be any constitutional office, without any accountability? When all the parties have held that Article 356 has been the most abused provision in either promulgating the President's Rule or in unduly protecting the party in power at the state-level, it is the political parties who have to collectively explain this malignancy that afflicted the umpires of the Constitution. It is this malignancy that has reduced umpiring into a sheer number game, as witnessed in the case of aborted imposition of

President's Rule in Bihar. It is the commissions and omissions of the political parties that have dented the functioning of the constitutional umpires.

Constitutional democracy is reduced to a number game as if democracy and Constitution are all about numbers. Once constitutional democracy is derailed due to poor umpiring standards, the nation gets paralysed. Governors recommending the imposition of President's Rule denying the duly elected parties the right to form the government on grounds that they were not able to cope with law and order (started in Kerala 1959); dismissing Chief Ministers instead of allowing the matter to be decided within the legislatures (started with West Bengal 1968); denial of opportunity to the parties in opposition to form Government (started in AP in 1954); and imposing President's Rule for a brief spell inorder to give a breather for flocking their sheep, (started in UP 1973), all of them together demonstrate how the Governors have brought down the image and efficacy of the august office. That they were coerced to do so by a superior force - the political force - amounts to betrayal of the Constitution, and of the solemnity of the oath of office.

The specific role assigned explicitly to the Governors by the Constitution in regard to matters such as tribal welfare and Tribes Advisory Councils has been diluted by all the political parties, to the point of neglect, due to the play of partisan factors. The Governors became mute witnesses to the situation. At the annual Governors' conferences, committees were set up to examine a number of issues such as the autonomy of universities and the role of governors as the chancellors. But nothing has come out of such initiatives. As the role efficacy and image got diluted and negated, there arose a number of occasions, when the public suggested abolition of the offices of governors. The emphasis at the

Governors' Conference 2003 that Governors must play a positive role, cannot be over emphasised.

Yet another distortion in the umpiring of the constitutional democracy is in regard to the judiciary. This impairment is witnessed in diverse dimensions and manifestations. With the vacuum in the political power process, arising from rampant foul-play by the political parties, the judiciary is getting loaded with an expanded role on a wide range of issues, with an ever increasing frequency. The second dimension is that the malignancies of the political process are creeping into the judicial sub-system in the form of coloured appointments, transfers, elevations, supersessions, and, even more, on a wide range of issues extraneous to the umpiring role.

The leadership of the legislative and the Judicial institutions have not succeeded in articulating and enforcing institutional discipline and in shaping standards of conduct and practices of the legislative and judicial institutions respectively. There are clear indications of popular awareness and concern about the diminishing standards of umpiring. When the leadership fails in shaping the institutions, the public generates pressure leading to the legislated mode of regulation.

Judiciary has diluted its own image as an umpire firstly by allowing its activism turning into extremism with a 'control-room' disposition towards the political and administrative organisations and personnel, but even more dangerously allowed to distort, its Judgements through a series of commissions, omissions and contemptuous statements by ill-motivated politicians. If the bureaucrats silently sabotaged, the power hungry politicians had tried to capitalise through open defiance of the judiciary. In a landmark judgement (10 May 1995) the Supreme

Court had asked the executive to implement Article 44 of the Constitution inorder to secure for the citizens a uniform civil code throughout the territory of India. While the political executive has maintained a stoic silence, the All India Muslim Personal Law Board (AIMPLB) called for the deletion of Article 44 of the Constitution, or the incorporation of a clause exempting the Muslims and others such as the Tribals, the Dalits and other minorities. A Muslim MP and leader of a political party expressed his reaction in the most contemptuous best : "it is no business of the judiciary to legislate . . . . to sit in Judgement over the Muslim Personal Law". . . . the way the Court has argued its case shows there is certain mentality behind it, certain motivation behind it . . . Argument of the Apex Court - - - - is a stupid argument" [4].

State governments have started showing scant respect to the judgements of the Supreme Court. It goes to the credit of the demos of the Republic that the image of the court, sullied by the political process, has survived, to date. But when members of the 'higher' judiciary sully their own image, as it happened when 26 Judges of Punjab and Haryana High Court proceeded on leave (19 April 2004) as a protest against the Chief Justice's "notices" to two sitting Judges regarding their "honorary" membership of a club, none else can save the sliding image.[5] And with the image goes the public esteem and functional efficacy as umpires of the constitutional game.

That the higher courts have started playing to the galleries is explicitly evident from the observations of the Supreme Court, that the High Courts should not play to the gallery or care for any applause from anyone or even need to take cudgels against any one making unnecessary remarks.[6] Even while dealing with recalcitrant subordinate Judicial officers, the Supreme Court had advised restraint.

Umpiring has suffered most due to one significant reason, that is, for a variety of historical factors, the Constitution of India has been projected and debated as if it is a legal document pure and simple, rather than as a political document. The consequence is that several serious issues of debate have been taken to the court of the Judiciary, while the sovereign Parliament, the people's court remained a mute witness. This process was aided and accentuated by the fact that the legislatures debated issues of constitutional significance with partisan dispositions, rather than as issues of common concern. In fact, most of the constitutional amendments were initiated in an atmosphere of partisan agenda , and political 'confrontation'.

Much of the constitutional deficit has arisen due to an unsettled and unsettling *inter-se* equations between the legislative, the executive and judicial institutions, due to the diverse dispositions of a 'power-play'. The process of 'checks and balances', which was at work until the Constitution came into being has not been appropriately adapted in terms of 'complementatiry of tasks and commonality of objectives' – one of the cardinal design parameters of the Constitution. In such a situation, the deficiencies of political and administrative processes have created a 'vacuum of power'; it is this vacuum that the judicial institutions seek to fill up. It was the political malignancy that has been described as the single greatest impediment to social transformation. The expressions and descriptions such as "change agents" and "catalysts" ascribed to the administrators had ceased to operate to such an extent that atleast two Chief Ministers publicly suggested to the citizens to beat up the administrators who do not perform but create impediments. It was in this context that people had turned to the judiciary by innovating an entry point in the form of Public Interest Litigation (PIL).

Public Interest Litigation has evolved into Judicial activism. When the political and executive processes continued to operate under conditions of constitutional insensitivity, with the deficiencies in umpiring added, Judicial activism has spread and assumed the proportions of extremism. Extremism in the sense that instead of correcting restoring and directing the political and executive actions, the judiciary has assumed direct (executive) control over administrative institutions and political processes. As the Judiciary itself has not attuned itself to the citizens' demands and constitutional parameters of delivery of justice, activism and extremism have not helped buttress the image of judiciary in a sustainable manner. "The ultimate reason for any type of judicial discipline is to maintain public confidence in the judiciary. The logic behind this principle is simple : A legal system can function only as long as the public accepts and abides by decisions rendered by the courts; the public will accept and abide by these decisions only if it is convinced that the judges are fair and impartial; anything that tends to weaken that conviction should be avoided. For this reason, judges are commanded to avoid not only actual impropriety but also the appearance of impropriety in all their activities".[7]

In India the 'contempt' jurisdiction of the legislatures and the judiciary ran parallel for long, in damaging the image of both. It is time that all the 'privileged' functionaries recognise that the people have conferred a set of privileges so as to ensure their performance "without fear or favour". There is no other facet of the judicial system that has earned for itself so much disrepute as the so called judicial commissions. These commissions have long been "reduced to a farce" as a former Chief Justice of India has put it, almost like a confessional statement. If the political, legislative and executive institutions had used, misused and abused the commissions over a period of time, the Judiciary has also contributed to this loss of credibility by allowing the situation to deteriorate. Public discourse on Judicial corruption, at the individual level, has remained a taboo for long years. Such a benign negligence, for long, both by the Judicial leadership and the legislatures has brought down its image, and attitude of the public towards the Judiciary.

The setting up of the National Commission for a Review of the Working of the Constitution (2000) demonstrated how even a review commission, its composition and terms of reference have been seen within a partisan frame rather than as a national concern warranting a consensual approach, and a grand national debate involving the demos. As the popular perceptions have been kept out of the review process, the partisan process has taken away the best of national concerns; a national exercise has been reduced to a notional one.

An independent, efficient, federal judiciary is a *sine qua non* for sustaining federalism. Our Supreme Court has, admittedly, developed several weaknesses at the expense of some of its federal attributes and status. It has to reestablish itself in terms of a commitment to federal constitutional values and creatively contribute to the process. Supreme Court is not merely the keeper of the letter of the Constitution, but also presents itself as the constitutional conscience keeper of the nation. A court can review and overrule its own judgements. But it cannot undo its wavering moments, for they get imprinted on the pages of history.

Federal relations in India are affected as much by the non-functioning or mal-functioning of the pre-existing provisions of the Constitution, as by the subsequent amendments. Several instances of states boycotting the state-run TV and Radio, West Bengal Assembly adopting a motion (1989) asking the Centre to stop blatant misuse of the Government monopoly media for propaganda purpose. Doordarshan's censor and/or refusal to telecast Chief Ministers' Independence Day and other messages, demand for the second channel on the TV for States, and admission by the Supreme Court of a writ petition (July 1989) challenging the Central Government's control over and monopoly of the broadcasting media and the manner of its functioning, are instances and illustrative areas of friction between the Centre and States in India. The number of Bills passed by States, run by political parties other than the one at the Centre awaiting Presidential clearance has been increasing, the duration of pendency of such bills at the Centre fluctuating.

As the constitutional machinery gets afflicted, the virus spreads all over the large network of regulatory mechanisms and autonomous institutions. This cancerous growth is best illustrated, in its worst form, in the case of stock-market scam due to manipulations like diversion of funds and fraudulent use of bank funds as observed by the Joint Parliamentary Committee (JPC:1992). What is more distressing to the people is that the JPC (2001) observed that lack of action on the JPC report of 1992 scam emboldened the wrong doers. "The special cell constituted to investigate the nexus between - - - - - - - - - - has gone defunct for years". The JPC 2001 observed that "this scam is basically the manipulation of the capital markets to benefit market operators, brokers, corporate entities and their promotees and managements". The JPC has reportedly pulled up the SEBI, and the Reserve Bank of India, another institution given a constitutional role and status. We have created a large network of regulatory mechanisms in the wake of liberalisation – but within a brief time almost all of them proved the need to reorganise and reorient themselves.

One of the former Presidents of India had observed within a month of his retirement that "as a President, I have often felt helpless, when so many delegations come to me and tell their woes and I can't do anything about it. Gujarat was a major example of helplessness", he said. Who else can feel helpful when the first citizen of the nation, who is assigned the role of 'protecting and defending' the Constitution feels and expresses helplessness? Helpfully, he himself quickly added that "To protect our society, when it is in danger, the President has a role to play".[8] Such a sacred role cannot be reserved for post-retirement reflections. The Presidents have to activate themselves, while in office, to preserve, protect and defend the sanctity of constitutional democracy in India.

President A.P.J. Abdul Kalam sent back to the cabinet for reconsideration of an ordinance seeking to negate an Election Commission circular asking every candidate standing for elections to the state and national legislatures to submit information regarding trials, prosecutions and concluded criminal cases against them apart from information on their assets along with their nomination forms. Once again, President A.P.J. Abdul Kalam has acted well within the parameters of his role in seeking a report from the Union Home Ministry. The letter of the Constitution does not explicitly confer such "powers" to the President, but the Constitution reposes the overarching role of preserving, protecting and defending the Constitution. The President cannot remain as a mute witness when the constitutional ethic is transgressed by the constitutional functionaries.

The constitutional deficit can be explained in terms of a few inherent deficiencies, but the problem cannot be explained fully unless the adjunct question is flagged : who has failed the Constitution? In the ultimate analysis, as Dr. Radhakrishna has observed : "A free India will be judged by the way in which it will serve the interests of the common man in the matter of food, clothing, shelter and the social services. Unless we destroy corruption in high places, root out every trace of nepotism, love of power, profiteering and blackmarketing which have spoiled the good name of this great country in recent times, we will not be able to raise the standards of efficiency in administration as well as in the production and distribution of the necessary goods of life".[9] If India fails its Constitution, it would deal a paralysing blow to democracy. Within five decades, we are already witness to a degradation in the quality of democracy, sliding towards increasing degrees of anarchy, as indicated in the Illustration 5.1. We have not been able to destroy the growing pyramid of corruption. The fact that we are creating a grand pyramid of pyramids (Illustration 3.6) in our flight against corruption reveals, in itself, a confession of deficiencies, if not failure. Institutional corruption, if unchecked, may assume the shape of a grand monument to the captivity of democracy in India.

Letter and Spirit

In the *pro forma* pursuit of the letter, we have missed the spirit of the Constitution. This is reflected, *inter alia,* in (a) high frequency of amendments to the Constitution, affected through a process of partisan and confrontationist game of numbers rather than democratic consensualism; (b) absence of an ethos of building conventions instead of rushing with amendments; (c) issue of ordinances at the pleasure

Illustration 5.1

MULTIPLE TRACKS OF SOCIAL TRANSFORMATION REFLECTING QUALITY OF DEMOCRACY AND FACTORS OF ANARCHY

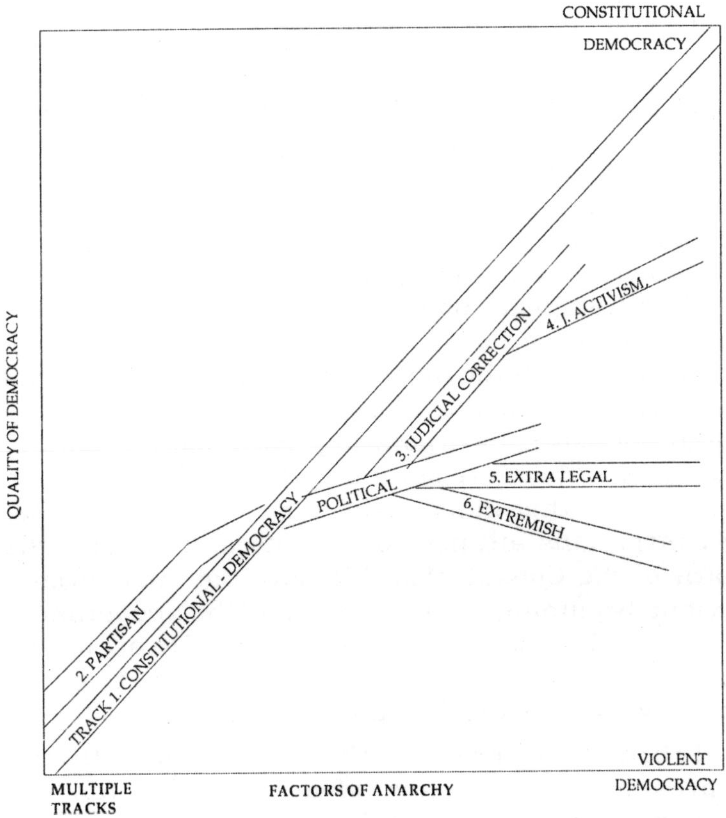

of political partisans; (d) absence of a mechanism to judge the judges and to promote autonomy and accountability of the judiciary; (e) absence of a recognizable measure of synergy among the instrumentalities, which are charged with complementary tasks; (f) generation and sponsoring of extra-constitutional forces and violent methods by the political parties and groups as a means to force extra-constitutional resolution of social (economic, political) conflict; (h) a leadership characterised by low levels of political morality, which does not share, much less subscribe to, the spirit and vision of the Constitution, and (i) absence of a sense of citizenship and nationalism among the people.

In five decades, India has amended the Constitution a hundred times, but has not promoted a set of constitutional conventions. Several Articles have been added, the preexisting ones modified or deleted with lightning rapidity, but we have not preserved and promoted the centrality of the Articles of faith viz., the Preamble and the Directive Principles. We had trampled upon the spirit of the Constitution on many an occasion. In the five decades, we had acted on many of the Amendments brought about with fan-fare. Though the Constitution of India is very comprehensive, incorporating many conventions of the British, there are several undefined areas. It is in this respect that India ought to have developed a set of conventions attuned to promote and sustain the spirit of the Constitution. We have not made even a serious beginning on issues such as the appointment of Prime Minister, President's discretion to act on the advise of the Prime Minister and his Cabinet, and in areas where the Constitution is silent.

Inorder to ensure that the Constitution representing the vision of a nation, yields the intended results, the spirit should be accorded significance, and reflected in terms of (a) democratic ethos and political morality, and (b) the conventions and traditions of the Constitution, cultivated and preserved as a habit.

Alongside the debasement of the democratic electoral process, and the emergence of extra-constitutional forces, we have cultivated dynastic dispositions. The greater danger of usurpation of power through manipulation and 'marketisation' of politics looms large as a threat to the constitutional democratic ethos of India.

The legislative conduct and performance are afflicted by a combination of practices such as contemptuous absenteeism, abstentions, walkouts, jumping into the well of the legislatures (as a pure and simple obstructionist tactic), creating obnoxious scenes, and exchange of unparliamentary epithets. The degradation of legislative behaviour has caused extensive damage to the process of constitutional democratic consensualism. The live coverage of the proceedings of legislatures on television has not helped the image of democracy in India. The citizens are witness to several resolutions unanimously adopted, committees set up to enhance the quality of parliamentary debate, and formulation of codes of conduct and ethics *ad nauseam*. Indians have yet to see a halt to degeneration before hoping for the retrieval of the democratic character of political parties and legislative conduct of elected representatives.

Political morality is at a low ebb. The largest democracy is hinged on contrived majority of numbers present and voting, as though numbers is all there is to democracy. Such a majority sought to legitimise even 'heinous crimes, against democracy' on several occasions. We are past the stage of corrupt individuals and corrupt political parties. Today the entire system stands corrupted.

The Members of *Rajya Sabha* expressed, on several occasions, concern at the increasing lobbying by certain financial institutions and industrial houses within the precincts of the Parliament House. Members said that the parliament house corridors were full of strangers, who were neither members nor the staff of the Parliament. One member cautioned that he came across some permanent faces at the reception and said that these were the people who were here to lobby for their bosses. The meaning, methods and modes of lobbying have lost their democratic sanctity. A member of the CPI said he had information that representatives of some financial institutions, both Indian and foreign, were present in the parliament house to gather 'information' for their respective organisations. There had been instances that these people had influenced some of the questions that came up before the House.

The working of a constitution does not depend wholly upon the nature of the Constitution. The factors on which the working of the organs of the state depend are (a) the people, and (b) the political parties that the people will set up as the instruments to carry out their wishes and their policies. That was the spirit of liberal democracy and the vision of 348 member-statesmen of India's Constituent Assembly. They had undertaken a pledge that "unless and until each Indian breathes the air of freedom and his miseries are banished and his hard lot is improved, our task remains unfinished". They were then engaged in a creative interaction for 165 days spread over almost three years in crafting 395 Articles and eight Schedules, through the process of consensus. But as Dr. Ambedkar observed "who can say how the people of India and their (political) parties will behave"?[10]

The gap between hope and reality was reflected by one of the outspoken members of the Constituent Assembly, four decades after India's constitutional democracy was set in motion. It was Minoo Masani who observed : "when we framed the Constitution of India, we made a sad mistake and thought that we were drafting a Constitution for English gentlemen. Unfortunately we had not bargained for the kind of politicians India has been suffering from for the last forty years. The Constitution is good, but we Indians let down".[11] The 'letter' of the Constitution cannot sustain itself and survive without the 'spirit'. It is only when the society protects both the letter and the spirit, its constitution survives and flourishes. The Constitution and the society have a reciprocal relationship.

Alarmed by the rebellion of 1857, the British Government empowered the Governor General, under the Indian Councils Act of 1861, to promulgate Ordinances for ensuring peace and good governance, when the legislature was not in session. Inspite of such empowerment, even an alien ruler like Lord Reading as the then Viceroy said : "I was almost staggered to find that I had the power to issue an edict, which could override the law of the land and every statuete passed in the land, and could not be discussed unless I allowed it". The Constitution provides for the promulgation of an Ordinance by the President when any matter calls for immediate action when the Parliament is not in session. But the democratic Government of India took to the Ordinance *raj* with such ease that during the period 1950-84 as many as 348 ordinances were issued, according to a Lok Sabha Secretariat Publication (1985) on Presidential Ordinances 1950-84. States have been even more indiscriminate, making light of the Constitution, in issuing ordinances in a frivolous manner, as illustrated by Uttar Pradesh which issued an ordinance to prevent students from 'copying' in examinations. Some state governments promulgated the same ordinances again and again. In Bihar alone, 256 ordinances were kept in force for periods ranging from one to 14 years. The Union Government did not set standards, but acted as a trend-setter. In 1994 alone, it promulgated 35 ordinances, an average of one for every ten days.

The ease with which ordinances were issued has led to the most appropriate yet atrocious expression "Ordinance *Raj*". This was indulged in by all the parties while in power, all of them turned bitter critics of ordinances while sitting on the opposition benches. It is this dilution in the conventions and traditions of constitutional democracy that prompted Nani Palkhivala to say : "the letter of the Constitution is satisfied by the President or the Governor, making a declaration that while the legislature is not in session, circumstances exist which render it necessary for him to take immediate action. The President as well as Governors are bound to act on the advice of the Council of Ministers who are jubilantly aware that outraging the sanctity of the Constitution, however shamelessly, is not a punishable crime".[12]

An independent, efficient judiciary is a *sine qua non* for sustaining the spirit of the Constitution. Our Supreme Court has admittedly developed several weaknesses at the expense of some of its federal attributes and status. It has to re-establish itself in terms of a commitment to the spirit of constitutional values, and creatively contribute to the process. The Supreme Court is not merely the keeper of the letter of the Constitution, but also the constitutional conscience of the nation. That is why it is given the constitutional mandate to review and overrule its own judgements.

The President, the Governors, the Speakers and Chairpersons of the Councils, the higher judiciary, every individual Members of Parliament and of legislatures, and the all India services were constitutionally equipped to operate within the framework of complementarity. Yet, as B.K. Nehru observed, "they have, however, in actual practice, not proved to be as effective as they were intended to be".[13] Observing that public esteem is a product of belief in the impartiality of constitutional functionaries, B.K. Nehru reflects on the changes in the public images of the character of Presidency thus : "The character of the presidency also underwent a change. Our first president Dr. Rajendra Prasad, although a politician, had in effect retired from politics and had no political ambitions. The second and third Presidents Dr. Radhakrishnan and Dr. Zakir Hussain had never been politicians. It was from the fourth presidency onwards that practicing politicians, who continued to take an active interest in political affairs, started being elected to office. The consequence was that the advice of the President ceased to be impartial or at least appeared to the general public to have ceased to be so. If the President belongs to the same political party as the Prime Minister, it is difficult for him to differ from somebody who is, in the party hierarchy, more important than he is. If he belongs to a different party (as has happened twice) his advice is suspect".[14]

Puzzled by the argument that the President can do nothing except on the advice of the prime minister, Minoo Masani, one of the articulate and outspoken members of the Consembly observed : "when the Constitution says that the Prime Minister and the cabinet hold office "during the pleasure of the President" what we meant was that they would hold office at their own pleasure! Can we imagine any Prime Minister going to the President and saying : "Sir, I advise you to dismiss me and my cabinet"? Similarly, if the President on his own, would have to call the Prime Minister, who has taken the trouble to pass the Bill through the two houses of parliament, and ask the Prime Minister to advice him to withhold assent for the same Bill. The question that arises is why is it so difficult for many people in this country to accept the language of the Constitution? Obviously it goes against some basic prejudice of theirs".[15] Perhaps, the spirit of the Constitution would be better appreciated if the issue is formulated in terms of the "role" of the President as the constitutional conscience keeper, protecting and defending the letter as much as the spirit of the Constitution, rather than in terms of his "powers".

The constitutional scope of synergy between the legislative and judicial institutions can be explored in three directions : (a) in the construction of the preambular concepts that contribute to a clear and unified vision of the nation; (b) sharing of common concerns in the management of the Judicial system; and (c) resolution of possible conflict of roles between themselves. It can be stated without fear of contradiction that the legislative and the judicial institutions have not evolved a clear and an integrated view of some of the preambular concepts. On the other hand there are wide gaps in their perceptions with the result that the vision of the Republic has not attained a steady state. While it is open to the judicial institutions to review their own decisions, the precedent of retired justices distancing themselves, or retracting from their own verdicts has not helped the process of a unified vision of the Constitution. The glaring variations in the perceptions and dispositions of the legislative and judicial institutions have only fractured the constitutional design for convergence, and accentuated the role-conflict. Even if the "basic structure" postulate enunciated by the Supreme Court is seen as a significant contribution, it defies any rational explanation as to how the concepts of socialism and secularism, that were not existing at the starting-line but interpolated later in the day, could become a component of the "basic structure".

The mutual dispositions of the legislative and the judicial leadership towards complementarity of their roles is illustrated by one of this author's professional experiences. In the face of the intense role-conflict between the legislative and judicial institutions – leading to collusion and deadlock, and locking of horns, this author had silently assumed the role of a concerned citizen and explored with three successive Speakers of the Lok Sabha, and three successive Chief Justices of the Supreme Court, during the period 1989-94, possible opportunities for a resolution of the conflict of roles through a creative, exploratory and informal interaction, without the media glare. The divergent responses revealed their widely varying patterns of dispositions. All the three successive Speakers had indicated that an informal creative interaction will be useful and should be explored. All the three successive Chief Justices of India on the other hand had indicated that the differences and areas of conflict could be resolved only in the highest judicial forum i.e. the Supreme Court. These responses, though patterned, do not lend themselves to any generalisations or firm conclusions, for all times. In the face of such unsettled dispositions and "power" orientations, the 'spirit' of synergy embedded in the Constitution gets debilitated. Their respective jurisdictions, relative autonomy, and accountability to the Republic are riddled with uncertainties and potential conflict.

Policies and procedures regarding the appointment, transfer, elevation or supersession, salary structure and infrastructure facilities on the one hand, and judging the judges covering aspects such as discipline, conduct and corruption on the other, constitute the common concerns of both the legislative and the judicial leadership. The growing hiatus and dissonance between the legislative and the judicial institutions is a matter of concern to the public. "In 1950 when the Constitution came into existence and till the 1980s, it was the executive which appointed the judges, and we have seen outstanding judges during that time. The question is of attitude. The Constitution was misused by the executive when the judiciary failed the nation, therefore people started getting suspicious".[16]

Social change is eternal in human society. Inorder to bring about directed change through socio-legal engineering, with legitimacy and credibility, we need legislative, executive and judicial institutions. The nature and degree of complementarity between them determines the quality, sustainability and pace of change. Any leverage gained by the extra-constitutional forces, in bringing about even the intended social change would, to that extent, erode the credibility of these institutions. Non-functioning or mal-functioning of constitutional institutions and provisions as much as the extra-constitutional processes have had an adverse impact on the conventions of the Constitution, and convergence of the institutions.

We seem to have lost sight of the fact that constitutional amendments stand on an entirely different footing than the amendments to ordinary legislation. It was in this context Dr. Ambedkar's observation that "parliament will have an axe to grind while the Constituent Assembly has none", assumes significance. The heights, nay the depths to which the constitutional culture has been debased was revealed in the proposal to amend the Constitution to prevent the abuse of the Constitution.

Very few attempts have been made to capture the vision and pursuit of action on a mission mode of governance. The first experiment in this direction that proved a success, was the green revolution. The success was entirely due to the nature and degree of complementarity and convergence of the political, the bureaucratic and the technocratic process in pursuing the vision of self-sufficiency in food production. The mission mode adopted in space technology has yielded significant yield. Two more experimental innovations stand out. One was the Mission Technology initiated and pursued successfully by Rajiv Gandhi as the Prime Minister. This mission mode of governance has not been consolidated and internalised due to a wide range of political and historical factors.[17] The second experiment was the vision strategy formulated by the Chief Minister of Andhra Pradesh Chandrababu Naidu. The nation has to analyse these experiments and experiences. There are many more instances and practices innovated and internalised without the explicit label. Institutions of state can learn from these practices and internalise the mission-mode of governance.

Democracy has the built-in advantage of self correction for it does not attain a static or frosen state, but assumes a live and evolutionary state. In fact the evolutionary character of democracy is nurtured by conventions and traditions, as much as by the culture and spirit of the Constitution. In the context of India, the Constitution has been crafted to sustain this evolutionary character. The Preambular statement sets out the primordial values, that constitute the pole-star, constantly guiding our Republican journey. The Directive Principles similarly inspire the quality of social transformation in the direction of the preambular pole star. They are designed to inspire and shape the process of public policy. There cannot be any doubt that merely because they are not enforceable they can be trampled upon. Just as Mahatma Gandhi had sated, 'when in doubt, hold a talisman', similarly, whenever there is any doubt about the Articles of the Constitution, the legislators have to reflect upon the spirit of the Constitution embedded in the Preamble and the Directive Principles. While the Supreme Court has been assigned the role of arbiter and interpreter, with advisory Jurisdiction on the letter of the Constitution, the President is assigned the sacred and ultimate task of preserving, protecting and defending the letter and spirit of the Constitution. The powers and authority vested in the Supreme Court thus do not impinge upon the 'role' assigned to the President as the overarching preserver, protector and defender of the Constitution.

It was unfortunate that the letter and the spirit were mixed up by superimposing transient dogma (such as 'socialism') in a frosen form, on the Preambular statement. It was equally unsustainable that the Judiciary endorsed this superimposition and went further to state that they constitute the 'basic immutable, features of the constitutional structure. The Supreme Court will, hopefully, review and revise its own opinion, sooner than latter; and thus help our democratic Republic uphold the spirit over the letter of the Constitution. As one of the American Presidents, Thomas Jefferson observed : "I know of no safe depository of the ultimate powers of society but the people themselves; and if we think them not enlightened enough to exercise their control with a wholesome discretion, the remedy is not to take it from them but to inform their discretion".[18] The citizens of the Republic of India assert their sovereignty, and rest their hopes on the Constitution and the spirit of constitutionalism.

References

1. Ambedkar B.R, The Constitution and the Constituent Assembly, Responsive to the Debate Ibid, p. 178.
2. APJ Abdul Kalam, Access to Justice, The Hindu, Hyderabad, Apr. 26, 2003 p. 1.
3. Guy Soran.
4. Rashtriya Chetana Vol. & 02 No. 13 Jan 2004.
5. The Hindu, Hyderabad 20 Apr 2004.

6. The Hindu, Hyderabad 15 Apr 2004.
7. Report of the Panel of Referees to the Minnesota Court of Appeals in Justice John J Todd's case University of Baltimore Law Report No. 225 p. 227.
8. K.R. Narayan. The Hindu, Hyderabad, Aug. 13, 2002.
9. Radhakrishnan S. The Constitution and Constituent Assembly – ibid An Appeal for concord and Tolerance Aug. 14, 1947 p. 48.
10. Ambedkar BR. The Constitution and Constituent Assembly Reply to the Debate Nov. 25, 1949 p. 177.
11. Minoo Masani Powers of the President. Freedom First July 1987 Bombay p. 21.
12. Palkhivala, Nani.
13. Nehru BK. Checks and Balances, Seminar on Problems of Democracy. Leshe Sawhney Program Bangalore 1987. p. 7.
14. BK Nehru ibid p. 7-8.
15. Minoo Masani ibid p. 53.
16. BK Nehru ibid p.8.
17. GRS Rao, Technology Mission, Rajiv Gandhi Foundation, New Delhi 1996.
18. Thomas Jefferson

6
TRYST WITH DESTINY
Managing the Vision

This cursory 'social audit' exercise brings out one point clearly, that more than reforming or amending the Constitution, we need to mend our modes of thinking and patterns of behaviour in the management of our Republic in order to move in the direction of making the tryst with destiny. The vision and the path set out in the Constitution not only remain valid, but are also validated by the contemporary Indian and global experiences. As a citizen's endeavour in formulating a social audit statement, as an *aide memoir*, for a debate on the management of our constitutional democratic vision, a set of issues that emerged from the 'audit' are flagged here. They are neither mutually exclusive nor exhaustive. These issues focus on the initiatives that the citizens, including all those manning the political parties, and institutions of governance, as citizens first, have to commit themselves to inorder to strengthen the democratic character as a way of life, and move in the direction of the "tryst with destiny".

Constitutional amendments would be wasted unless we mend our methods first. Even a second Republic will not help us unless we mend ourselves first, and if we mend ourselves, we can transform our nation into a great developed and evolving democracy even without any amendments to the Constitution.

The constitutional vision has to be brought into full-play for which we have the capability – what is found inadequate is the will, political and administrative. The popular will has to be ignited, not negated. Democracy is a faith with the people of India. It can be sustained by dedicated and creative leadership, evenn without a Constitution. This is the challenge of change before the leadership of India.

The Constitution of India is more than a legal document, it encompasses, in letter and spirit, the political ethics of our democracy. The vision of India it presents is not trapped in the language. The language reflects and exudes the vision. In the Indian context, and of the newly emerging nations that have won their political freedom during the closing decades of 20th century. Indian Constitution defines, operationalises and lends meaning to political freedom, participative development, and democratic governance. Freedom is the elixir of life, as air is to human body. What is true of an individual is equally true of the 'collective' liberal values of freedom, freedom from subjugation, bondage, fear, and want; civil liberties; and socio-economic rights of citizens. The Constitution of India incorporates the universal human rights and the modus for the process, not for freesing democracy but for promoting democratisation. Freedom movement that has welded the multitude of diverse groups into the mainstream citizenship and national spirit, demonstrated the vital role of leadership with a vision, conviction and commitment. The visionary leadership did not have a 'constitution' inorder to promote and translate the vision of freedom and democracy. Gopala Krishna Gokhale often said that this generation was "destined to fail but that the success of the subsequent generations could be built on the foundations of his generation's failure".[1] The leadership of the freedom movement was dedicated to duty, not the fruits. That is how they had ignited the passion of the people, as Indians first and Indians last.

Reflecting on the Objectives Resolution in the Consembly, Jawaharlal Nehru said "I cannot say that this resolution at all conveys the passion that lies in the hearts and the minds of the Indian people today". "We have given the context of democracy – but the main thing is that in such a resolution – we would have put in something which may be agreeable to many but not agreeable to some – therefore, we have laid down, not theoretical words and formulae, but rather the content of the thing we desire".[2] A clear conviction that it is the spirit and the substance that prevail and triumph over mere language and declarations.

The fulfilment of India's tryst with destiny is determined by (1) internalisation of democratic tradition as a way of life, (2) sustained culture of constitutionalism, (3) human development as the qualitative micro-level index of nation-building, i.e. man as the measure of development, (4) good governance as the only reference point of Government, and (5) reclamation of civil society as the bulwark of democracy.

6.1. Restore Democratic Tradition Make it a Way of Life

Dr. Radhakrishnan cautioned the nation about the quality of leadership; "Our opportunities are great but let me warn you that when power outstrips ability, we will fall on evil days. We should develop competence and ability, which would help us utilise the opportunities, which are now open to us. From tomorrow we cannot throw the blame on the Britisher. We have to assume the responsibility ourselves for what we do. A free India would be judged by the way in which it will serve the interests of the common man in the matter of food, shelter and social activities".[3] Democratisation demands sustaining of a dynamic equilibrium under conditions of rapid change. Such social conditions and constitutional provisions have to mesh, establishing between themselves a dynamic equation. Constitution has been designed to generate, and to cope with an ever changing socio-economic scenario. Managing change is tough and in itself constitutes a challenge, negation is as easy as igniting a dynamite. That is why, democratic renewal and preservation and promotion of constitutional spirit are the two critical inputs in managing the vision of the Constitution of India. Any attempt to stifle the democratic spirit will bounce back leading to its resurgence, renewal and rejuvenation. Distortions imposed or attempted, operate as manna for the spirit of democracy.

The Constitution has merely launched the nation on the path of democracy and development. Whether the take-off is smooth, and trajectory is as per design parameters, or in need of mid-course corrections represent the role of mission-management, the role of government, and good governance.

Even within the span of the first five decades, the socio-political environment has impacted much more on the working of the Constitution than what the Constitution itself had attempted and succeeded in shaping the socio-political ground conditions. Democratisation calls for reinvestment of life into the basic process of power. The electoral process, which is the sustainer of democracy, is in dire need of quality check, assurance and nourishment. Providing statutory sanctity to the political parties and process, their incorporation, operation, management and public accountability is a *sine qua non*. Leaders were being worshipped, admired and followed by the millions during the freedom movement. Elected leaders were being referred to as *'vidhayaks'*, the makers of the destiny of people. Today's leaders have to restore that 'trust', lest, people's disdain for politicians might prompt them to destroy the political system, which will cause incalculable and irreparable damage to democracy in India. Lead life by example, not by privileges, immunities and a vulgar display of power. Today as the rest of the world has started appreciating the relevance of Gandhi, remember what he said : "My Swaraj is to keep intact the genius of our civilisation. I want to write many new things but they must be all written on the Indian slate"; and that "my resistance to Western civilisation is really a resistance to its indiscriminate and thoughtless imitation based on the assumption that Asiatics are fit only to copy everything that comes from the West".

In view of the abuses that have crept into the political system, it is important that measures to reform the political process are taken up as the desideratum. They are : (a) A law providing for the manner in which parties should be registered, adopt a constitution, prepare accounts, and subject them to audit and file suitable returns before a designated regulatory authority. Every political party must be required to have a constitution of its own and have the same registered with the said authority. (b) All parties should be required to maintain proper accounts of their income and expenditure, and the same subjected to audit by the prescribed authority; provisions of section 13 (a) of the Income Tax Act, (which require political parties to maintain proper accounts, etc. to get exemption from I.T. in respect of certain incomes) be rigidly followed with conviction and commitment, (c) the regulatory authority should have the responsibility to take action against any Party if it violates the provisions of registration, or does not maintain proper records and accounts. (d) Where a Party is found to have violated its constitution or the law or rules, it should be disqualified as a party. (e) Stringent preventive measures should be taken to check multiplicity of candidates, and to eliminate irresponsible candidates who do not take the election process seriously.

Democratic politics finds its meaning in the liberal thought of tolerance and multiculturism where "power has to be used within the framework of a moral and just order for the welfare of the people". We need to contain the high degree of fragmentation of society by providing a code of conduct and ethical parameters for political parties. These parameters would not only define their realm, but also promote accountability for their actions and performance, vis-a-vis promises.

Political process, by the very nature, has to perform the role of "harmoniser" of conflicting values, and interests while preserving the pluralist character of a democratic polity. It is the negation of political process if it contributes to social fragmentation on the basis of caste, region, religion and such other factors. Checks and safeguard need to be provided especially when the likely victims of political power are going to be the most vulnerable sections of the population. It is imperative then to make the rights guaranteed by Article 30 an affirmative one and prevent the danger of it becoming a tool of exploitation.

The rhetoric of reform has shifted its focus from the core to the peripheral issues, and, even worse, deception of democracy. Instead of measures to strengthen if not universalise, participation so as to promote the core value of democratic majority in the first place, and majority of votes polled next, political parties have started resorting to bogus enrolment in the bulk. The ideas of a fixed tenure, as well as the premature dissolution of a legislature sound obnoxious, measured by the standards of liberal democracy.

Dissolving an Assembly at the will of the political party that has formed the government, especially inorder to facilitate choosing the time favourable to the ruling party represents as anti-democratic as rigging the elections, and goes counter to the will of the people. When any party opts for dissolution, or defeated on the floor of the Assembly, the state Governor should take over the administration inorder to promote and protect administrative neutrality before and during the elections. Such a provision would curb the tendency of kite-flying, pursuit of partisan political advantage and financial stress and distress arising from illegal party-funds, frequently. India has monetisatised the democratic process to an extent that many candidates contest elections to raise enough resources that even if they are defeated at the hustings, they have already made enough money. Contesting elections from the confines of a prison, contesting from more than one constituency, and contesting to the national and state legislatures simultaneously will be repugnant to democracy. The Supreme Court's (interim) Order of 4 June 2004 restraining the Election Commission of India from issuing a notification to fill 65 vacancies in the *Rajya Sabha* on the basis of a petition challénging the amendments made to the Representation of the People Act 1951 [which dispensed with the requirement of domicile for the candidaes contesting the *Rajya Sabha* elections], threw up many issues of a more critical nature in the working of constitutional democracy in India. Some of them are : (a) political parties adversely affected the constitutional norm of Rajya Sabha as the Council of States; and (b) political parties collectively decided to debase the sanctity of vote by shifting secret ballot into an open ballot, out of purely partisan consideration. The Supreme Court Bench observed that if such an important question was put before it where the "basic structure" of the Constitution was alleged to have been altered, then it "is a fit case for interference".

Arrest the democratic slide, by a conscious recognition that when representatives cease to represent, it will defeat democracy and the resultant vacuum will be filled by anarchy; reinvest life (*Punah Prana Pratistha*) into India's body politic; arrest the 'Biharisation' of Indian polity and democracy before it crosses the point of no return. In short, restore the gravity of democracy back to the Parliament. Indian Parliament has to reinvest life into the political system, set standards for the state legislatures, and nurture respect for the democratic ethic in the *Panchayati Raj* institutions as the true foundation of democracy. Restore the image of a role-model of democracy as obtaining at the starting point of our constitutional parliamentary democracy.

A slide in the performance of Parliament manifest in the form of low productivity or non-performance can be considered normally as an inadequacy. No organisation of governance, business or of civil society can attain and retain 100 per cent efficiency, certainly not for all times. But, when any organisation reveals 'mal-functioning' it must be recognised as an 'emergency' situation. If a malfunction is detected but not attended to, in good time, it would be an invitation to disaster. The nation has been a witness to such malfunctioning of the legislative, the Judicial and the executive instrumentalities of state on several occasions. Any neglect or delay in the 'corrective' process would not merely burn-out the instruments, but, the mission of democracy itself would be at stake.

Decentralisation of structures and participation by the people constitute the two liberal attitudes, the two sides of the coin of democracy. In the Indian context the paradox is that at the starting line (1950) there existed, *de facto,* more decentralisation than after the constitutionally provided *de jure* decentralisation. The *de jure* decentralisation has been negated by (a) the frosen state of centralised bureaucracy and (b) 're-centralisation' of political leadership, institutions and process. "Freedom" from the British secured by the people is yet to be passed on to the 'people through decentralised structures and participative processes. Decentralisation as a process encompasses and gets reflected in all the facets of political, economic, social and cultural dimensions of a liberal democracy. It is only then that decentralisation and participation will fortify and fructify. Decentralisation has to be irrigated and channelised from *Lok Sabha* to *Gram Sabha.* Thus, decentralisation is yet to be transformed from the status of structures towards a process of participation. Such participation (empowerment, gender equity, *et al*) has to go beyond the much talked about PRIs to encompass all aspects such as 'community-policing', '*Nyaya Panchayats*', mutually-aided cooperatives, producers' market committees; and cultural organisations, not controlled by the state. Consensualism and commonality in place of the partisan pursuit of power are nurtured and sustained by the status and quality of the process of decentralisation. Where such a vital process of democracy is reversed, or stalled, there emerge resistance and counter-pressures in the form of 'federalism', 'reorganisation' of states, and myriad forms of resistance and extremism.

The life sustaining vital nourishment is being sucked away, in myriad ways by the political leaders. Three instances illustrate and warrant urgent consideration. The members of Parliament and of Legislatures sitting and dominating, if not dictating and destroying, the proceedings of *Panchayati Raj* institutions; the practice of appointing 'guardian' ministers of state cabinet as in-charge of districts; and Members of Parliament and of Legislatures' Local Area Development funds, while starving the PRIs of funds are sapping the vital life sustaining process of Indian democracy. Wisdom demands that these aberrations are curbed and cured in good time, at the level of political leadership before they move over to the Judicial fora in the form of public interest litigation.

A far more critical issue that could destroy the integration and integrity of the nation is the emergence of state-level political parties with a local agenda. Such local parties are collaborating to eject the national parties at the national level. A collation of regional parties contesting and winning a majority in the parliament can convert it into a "jungle-fare" with serious implications to democracy, national integrity and integration. This and several other similar issues should have been considered by the Commission to Review the working of the Constitution.

The constitution of India seeks to promote democracy as a way of life where law runs parallel to life. The spirit of constitutional democracy breathes through all the institutions of state; the institutional convergence is built through the constitutional architecture. They cannot neutralise each other for then they contribute to their collective atrophy. Constitutional consensualism cannot be seen as an expediency-political, economic, social or cultural but as an Article of faith in the liberal democracy of India. Rajaji's statement that "we must rebuild our lost aristocracy, not of birth or not of wealth or even of intellect, but of character" represents a vital ingredient of liberal democracy. United Kingdom has no written constitution, but over centuries, has accumulated the wisdom of practices, conventions and a tradition of respecting such norms and standards. Yet, it remains a model of democracy. In India, though we have an elaborately written Constitution, we have amended it a hundred times in fifty years; the number will exceed if all the attempted and aborted amendments are taken into consideration. A constitution is not to be frosen as immutable, but where partisan politicians mutilate the Constitution in the name of amendments, inorder to gain a momentary partisan advantage, the culture and tradition of constitutionalism get destroyed. Not all constitutional amendments make any sense after a lapse of time and, in fact they show how they were carried out purely to meet short – term political ends. As James Madison, the fourth President of the United States of America observed, "in framing a government, which is to be administered by men over men, the great difficulty lies in this : you must first enable the government to control the governed; and in the next place oblige it to control itself". [4]

The 'mis-alliance' of the legislative, executive and judicial 'powers' will lead to the tyranny of state. Where these operate in pursuit of constitutional goals, and in the spirit of constitution, their orientation will reflect in terms of institutional convergence and synergy in rendering service to the citizens. That is the spirit of constitutionalism. The spirit of constitutionalism would be protected and promoted by adopting non-legislative norms and conventions rather than resorting to instant amendments and excessive legislation matched by deadly inaction, corroding, in the process, the constitutional fundamental of the rule of law. That is how and why India has acquired the label of a functional anarchy.

6.2. Pronote Constitutionalism

Periodic Review and Reform

The Constitution of India is a consensual document. All the political parties and leaders of the day 'swear' by it in a declaratory fashion. The spirit of constitutionalism is better sustained by conforming, in action, to the constitutional intent and design. The 'sale' of membership, and induction of defeated candidates into *Rajya Sabha* with such rapid speed, individuals operating as chief ministers yet voting in the Parliament are not practices that would enhance the spirit of the Constitution. Certainly, they are not the practices that would enable India to move towards being a great democracy. Such acts, simply, constitute a contempt of citizens, and an affront to the Constitution.

When democracy is seen as a process, then citizen-education assumes centrality. It is the citizens who constitute the bulwark of democracy. In the Indian context, "we the people" are yet to be citizenised. Education for democracy is not the same as literacy levels. Education for democracy has to encompass all the people – the illiterate, poverty striken at one end, and the 'modernised' high-flying corporate executives at the other end of the spectrum so as to help all the citizens attain the minimal standards of 'citizenship', the discipline of democracy, nation-building, and national development.

The Constitution of India represents a pole-star that provides direction to the nation. It seeks to provide and sustain good governance, social harmony and national development, all at a time. Political process (parties and leadership) is assigned the task of socio-legal engineering, the task of servicing social transformation. However within the first few decades, as the political process turned malignant, the missionary role of political parties in managing the vision of the Constitution got distorted. The spirit of 'constitutionalism' got diluted as the parties started playing with the letter of the Constitution. The spirit of constitutionalism was substantially eroded by processes such as (a) redundant amendments, (b) abuse and disuse of Articles such as 356, (c) faulted appointments and abuse of constitutional positions for partisan ends, leading to (d) disfunctional institutions (e) consigning of legislative processes to the streets, leading to anarchic conditions, (f) the guardians turning into mute spectators as (g) the democratic process tended to lose its vital ingredient of 'discipline'.

The 73rd and 74th Amendments to the Constitution literally amount to a confession on the part of political parties that they have failed in promoting decentralisation and mobilising people's participation in the process of social transformation. Having made the amendments, retaining the bureaucratic structure, and centralisation in-tact, the political leaders had started the process of re-centralisation of power. It is a clear case of trampling upon the spirit of constitutionalism. This process pales into insignificance when viewed in the background of how easily the preamble itself has been amended, and the constitutional amendments have been placed on par with ordinary legislation.

No Article of the Constitution has been so mutilated by repeated misuse, abuse and disuse as Article 356, by all the parties. It reminds one of the story of 'crying wolf' meant for the children. Ultimately the nation became a mute witness to the helplessness of the Union Government and of the Parliament as the guardian of the Constitution when the wolf had, in fact, struck in Bihar. It is a travesty of constitutional democracy that the Chief Ministers Conference (Srinagar : 2003) was concerned about safeguard's against the possible abuse of Art 356, and ignored the concerns of national integrity and constitutional democracy. The political parties continued with their political agenda without caring for the spirit of the Constitution. It is time to prevent the 'Biharisation' of democracy in India.

Appointment of functionaries to Constitutional offices (such as the Governor, CAG, CEC, members of higher judiciary) should not be, and should not appear to be, the prerogative of any 'political party' in power. The process itself should be broad-based as to reflect consultation and consensus. Image, acceptability and propriety are as important as competence in the appointment of these functionaries. The position of Leader of the Opposition has to be strengthened by associating him / her with the process of appointments to constitutional offices so as to promote acceptability of incumbents even in a situation of fluctuating political fortunes. Trust reposed by the people in the constitutional offices and functionaries cannot be allowed to get eroded. Trustees, guardians and umpires with constitutional status cannot become partisans; certainly not usurpers and despots.

In India, the elected representatives have become a separate 'class', the 'ruling or political class' suborning all the shades of parties and ideology'. The most frequent and visible misuse and abuse of the office is that of Governor. The dignity of the Governor's office should be restored and its independence guarded by making him non-transferable; and, irremovable except by impeachment. The Governor is the Head of the State. He should not be transferred from one State to another. All correspondence with or by him should be routed through the President alone. In no case should any civil servant or, for the matter, Minister of the Union, deal with him directly. Instrument of instructions to guide the Governor in his duties should be embodied as conventions of the Constitution. It is of vital importance that the one principle recommended by the Administrative Reforms Commission, the Speakers' Conference, and the Sarkaria Commission, and accepted by all political parties should receive constitutional recognition; Where the Governcr has reason to believe that the Government has lost the confidence of the legislative assembly, he should suggest to the Chief Minister to summon the Assembly within a reasonable period inorder to secure a vote of confidence from the Assembly.

Political parties must stop taking issues of public concern to the streets, much less to the temples and mosques. They must stop generating conflict as a mechanism to gain and sustain power. They should take social agenda to the Parliament and legislatures and resolve them harmoniously. The primacy of Parliament must be restored so as to ensure that it helps maintain the gravity of democracy. What Ambedkar said on the sanctity of constitutionalism merits reiteration: "The first thing they must do is to hold fast to the constitutional methods of achieving their social and economic objectives and abandon the methods of civil disobedience, non-cooperation and *satyagraha* for these methods were nothing but the grammar of anarchy".[6] It is of no consequence if the guardians, trustees and national leadership introspect, post-facto. They must speak, and act in good time, in keeping with their role and responsibility as the keepers of the constitution. It is they who have to build conventions in good time, and sustain them, by preventing abuse.

Democracy can take roots, survive and flourish only when there is that vital force of discipline, at all levels, in all segments of the society. The overwhelming popular – will was demonstrated in the framing of the Constitution. There is an urgent need, a true emergency situation, for the political will to sustain the vision of the Constitution, failing which the political class will prove itself to be the *Mahishasura* of democracy. There are clear signs of rebellion by the younger generation; if it is neglected now, the country suffers. But, democratic forces and forms will emerge from the ashes of anarchy. The political class has the choice. The choice and its implications are very clear. Amendments to the Constitution should not be by the simple process of vote and abstention; the mode has to be consensual. It was in this context that Dr. Ambedkar said "Parliament will have an axe to grind while the Constituent Assembly has none".[5]

If we have the conventions rooted in the polity, we don't need even the Constitution, let alone amendments. If we don't have a firm faith in the democratic ethic, and nurture the conventions, even a second constitution can not protect and rescue our democracy. As to how even a review process can be subjected to partisan processes has been demonstrated by the National Committee for a Review of the Working of the Constitution (2000-2002). Review and reform of any constitution have to be a constant, as periodic exercises promotes democratic renewal, and nourishment to the body politic. In the case of India, constitutional democracy, good governance and social transformation are dynamically interrelated and hence review and reform acquire added significance in promoting a dynamic equilibrium. However, review and reform cannot be allowed to be based *ab initio* on partisan considerations, impulsive and dramatic in nature. Ideally, review and reform have to be at agreed, pre-determined intervals of time, to be undertaken with due process. An essential element of a review is informed public debate, especially involving the incoming generations. A review can not be based on either inclusion or exclusion of issues. Ideally, a commission has to be appointed by a resolution and in the Parliament, without reducing the focus or process to either juristic or forensic style. It has to be a holistic, creative process on the lines of a Round Table, not adversarial methods of a court-room. A constitutional review is not only a safety valve, but more a shock absorber, and a mechanism for real-time reform – that includes in its scope, *inter alia*, fine-tuning the Constitution to the ever-changing global, national and local socio-political scenario. In the case of India's constitutional democracy, a review came up as a golden opportunity. Unfortunately, the review became futile on several counts, most significantly on two. First, the citizens were not even aware of the constitution of a Review Commission, not to speak of consultation or participation in such a review. All this inspite of the fact that an overwhelming majority of people covered in a nation-wide study wanted, but did not get, an opportunity to participate. Second, the vision of the Constitution – the Preambular soul of the matter has been excluded from the review as a precondition for the chairman-nominee to accept the offer. Thus, the Chairman had deprived the nation of the benefit of the views of the members of the Commission on the 'basic structure' issue, an issue on which, the highest Judicial institution itself opined, that there is a need for crystallisation of the concept. The futility of the exercise was brought out by one of the members of the Commission, when he observed that several of the recommendations of the Commission went directly counter to the clear decisions of the Commission. It was a great national opportunity, frustrated and aborted by the Commission itself.

6.3. Accelerate Development

Focus on Human Development

As a nationalist poet Gurajada had stated, it is not a territory but the people that make a nation. Human development proceeds on two tracks which run parallel to each other. First is the material well-being and second the non-material social harmony and quality of life.

Material wellbeing, the process as well as status, should be based not merely in terms of macro Gross Development / National Product (GDP / GNP), or the averages such as the Standards of Living calculated in the aggregate, which may be useful but not adequate. According to the norms of liberal democracy, which is what the Indian Constitution envisions, material prosperity should be aimed at freedom from starvation, want, disease and the like, *Sarvodaya* and *Antyodaya,* the philosophical ideals of welfare of all, including the last-man in the que. Standards of living of individuals have to be attuned to meet the quality of life of the community as a whole; must meet the criterion of the talisman given by the Father of the Nation. Capitalism, market-economy, socialism, socialistic pattern, liberalisation or globalisation *et al* represent the transient dogma; they should not be allowed to lead to the consequences of exclusion and alienation if not both on the part of people. Material growth attuned to human welfare operates devoid of dogma, promotes liberal democratic values such as dignity of labour, sense of identity, inclusion and responsible and responsive citizenship.

The non-material socio-cultural stream takes in its stride liberal democratic ideals that help harmonise the conflict of values, fuse together the diverse identities, and harmonise the competing interests. Thus the 'non-material cultural process calls for socio-legal engineering in tune with the architectural vision of the Indian constitution – peace, harmony and development, promoting citizenship and national spirit, in an ambience of the family of man, *Vasudhaiva Kutumbakam.*

Education in its quintessential and comprehensive sense operates as a trigger and a multiplier of social transformation; (a) assured livelihoods and dignity of labour; (b) promotion of pluralism as an essential value of liberal democracy; (c) tolerance and freedom; and (d) people-centered mode of mobilisation for social reform and transformation. Swami Vivekananda observed : "All the wealth of the world can not help one little Indian village if the people are not taught to help themselves". He pleaded for "bringing light to the ignorant, and more light to the educated for the vanities of the education of our times are tremendous. True and liberal education should and would help build a society free from bigotry, fundamentalism and extremism".[6]

The United Nations has recognised, at the global level, three basic aspects of human development not isolated from each other : longevity, knowledge and a decent standard of living. Longevity is measured by life expectancy at birth; knowledge is measured by a combination of the adult literacy rate and the combined primary, secondary and tertiary gross enrolment ratio and standard of living by GDP per capita. But the HDI does not measure or even reflect the indices such as political participation or gender inequities which constitute the dimension of democracy index as an adjunct to developmental index. The Human Development Report (HDR) 2003 has thus focussed on the Millennium Developmental Goals – which are reflected in the Constitution of India which was formulated in 1950; Indian democracy represents a case of five decades ahead in articulating the Millenial Developmental Goals formulated and presented in HDR 2003.

Issues of measurement related to these factors demonstrate the conceptual and methodological challenges that remain to be tackled. It represents a challenge and an opportunity to formulate a composite democracy index and the method of its measurement. The Millennial Development Goals (MDG) set out by the HDR 2003 are : (1) eradication of extreme poverty and hunger; (2) achievement of universal primary education; (3) promotion of gender equity and empowerment of women; (4) reduction of child-mortality; (5) improvement of material health; (6) combating HIV/AIDS, malaria and other disease; (7) ensuring environmental sustainability, and (8) development of a global partnership for development.

These elements of human development are not only in tune with the Constitution of India, but also the lessons learnt from the diverse experiments in development all over the global communities during the 20th century. "Sustainable development is that development which meets the needs of the present without compromising the ability of future generations to meet their own needs. This means avoiding the accumulation of environmental debts (by polluting or exhausting natural resources) as well as financial debts (through unsustainable borrowings), social debts (by neglecting to invest in human development) and demographic debts (by permitting unchecked population growth or urbanisation). Human development must allow each generation balance its budget in each of these four areas".[7]

Indian Constitution deals with civilisational issues of democracy and development. The great social thinker Margaret Mead observed : "In each age, there is a series of pressing questions which must be asked and answered. On the correctness of the question depends the survival of those who ask. On the quality of the answers depends the quality of life these survivors will lead".[8]

Democracy is not merely 'decentralised-participatory-mode' of managing the affairs of a polity, it is an integral part of development; democracy and development have to be integrated, merged and fused. Such development has to be tested against the Directive Principles on the ground, not in the court-room.

It is only as a matter of sheer operational feasibility that the civil and political rights are categorised as Fundamental Rights, and the socio-economic rights as the Directive Principles. It is only an issue of sequencing; non-justiciability does not free the polity from accountability to the people's court, for going against the Directive Principles.

Reconstruction of the human condition is a *sine qua non* for social reconstruction. But if we start with economic reconstruction without consciously attuning it to human reconstruction, it would be a sure recipe for social dissonance. As Minoo Masani observed " if it was true in the time of Abraham Lincoln that no nation could be half slave and half free, it is equally true today in this shrinking world that we cannot have a world that is half slave and half free".[9]

Democratic social transformation is a complex, yet fascinating process. Indian Constitution provides for a wide spectrum of change, under conditions of relative stability; it attempts to promote revolutionary change in an evolutionary mode. There is a cyclical relationship between the change ignited by the Constitution; and the reciprocal impact of such changes on the constitutional process. Such process encompasses contra-indicators, reflected in sum as factors of Gross Social Conflict (GSC) emerging from the pattern and process of change. Hence, the universally recognised desirability of having a

Commission on Social Development at the level of the United Nations, at the national levels; and, in large pluralist countries like India, at local levels too.

When a pluralist polity with historical hangovers, tries to forge ahead, there will be conflicts. Recognition and reinforcement of the fact that all problems can be resolved, as we did manage on several occasions in our post-independence era, is a vital process of change. This is a function of leadership of the nation. Politics and politicians are necessary for the functioning of a democracy inorder to mobilise, organise and represent the will of the people. We had the benefit of a Vivekananda , a Tagore, a Gandhi, a Bhabha, a Nehru, a Lok Nayak, a Balagangadhar Tilak, who stirred the people as a resource is making significant contributions to the development of our nation in diverse fields. We have a living legend of visionaries, today. Indians had for long made, and continue to make, significant contributions beyond the shores of India. How come we are faced with a situation, in the words of CR, "we have to restore the aristocracy of moral/political leadership". The fact of the matter is we have simply neglected the need to invest in and infuse political morality of service to the people. Is it not Gandhi, the Mahatma who said "serving the millions of Indians constitutes my politics?

As democracy represents a consensual mode, today we need conscientious leaders. The issue of minorities has been resolved by the Consembly by common agreement, through a consensual process, in a manner satisfactory to the various interests involved. National integration constitutes a *sine qua non* for the integrity of a pluralist polity comprising of a plethora of religious, linguistic and ethnic groups. In such a situation, secularism has been perceived and placed on par with pluralism, and as an ethic of democracy but not in terms of numerical majorities or minorities, or as a postulate pitted against religion. Integration, harmony and pluralism have been seen as the quintessential attributes of liberal democracy. That is how the democratic ethic has been sought to be sustained not in terms of an asserting majority and a dissenting minority. This liberal disposition has been strengthened by the charter of Fundamental Rights as vital for a democratic polity and good governance.

6.4. Promote Good Governance
People Centric Mission Mode

Governance is the process of translating the meaning and fulfilment of democracy. Democratic governance which is what constitutes the mode of the Constitution of India can not be confined to a mere 'representative' form, but has to be tempered by the substance of decentralised structures and participative processes. Democratisation of governance is not merely a process requirement; it lends substance to the process of governance. Democratisation and social transformation are not as simple as administering an operational manual. It is a dynamic process of awakening, empowering, channelising, involving, absorbing and harmonising. It is a process that involves both ends and means, methods and substance, encompasses defining, designing and reengineering, inducting adequate and appropriate systems; and, most important of all, infusing an ethic of rendering service with dedication and devotion.

To this end the pre-existing administration, with its status and *status-quo* orientation has to be reengineered to reflect the values of liberal democracy and participative ethos, in the service of the sovereign people of India. Administration has to shed off its Weberian characteristics of centralisation of power and hierarchical-control orientations. It has to operate as the instrument of social transformation. Decentralisation implies and encompasses openness, access and involvement of people (empowerment), and internalisation in a democratic ethic. Proliferation of the structures of state counters decentralisation and participation. Government has to compress itself in sise and facilitate more and more of efficient, effective and productive governance.

As the government expands, the quality of governance goes down; corruption and atrophy afflict the quality of governance. The expansion has only contributed to an all-pervasive conflict in myriad forms such as centre-versus-state, legislature versus judiciary, elected versus appointed executive, IAS versus IPS, generalist versus specialist *et al.* This bureaucratic mase has impeded the emergence of responsible citizenship, and created levels of corruption that has generated citizen alienation and hostility. What is needed is a convergence and synergy. The induction of information and technological (ITC) innovations into the process of governance has not enhanced transparency and accountability; ITC has often been adapted to accentuate centralised authoritarian dispositions.

The plethora of exercises in reform – political, legislative, judicial, executive and regulatory – have yielded rich guidelines. What is needed is the will of the leadership of all these institutions, recognising that all these functionaries are, in the first place, the citizens of this country. Reform initiatives, thus far, did not even remain cosmetic, they had only added to the layers, units and bulk, as a dead weight on the Republic. An occasional serious, self-critical introspection reveals that individual initiatives and redesign of the structures go together, not in isolation or in sequence. Quality of service to the people, the sovereign authority in a democracy, constitutes the touchstone of performance. Governments can not provide solutions in situations where they themselves constitute the problem.

Corruption has emerged as the single largest threat to constitutional democracy in India. Starting as an individual aberration in a sporadic manner the virus, left unchecked, has debilitated the system of governance, and now in an epidemic form has engulfed the entire polity. Money, crime and power have coalesced to enervate the constitutional democracy in India. The anti-corruption methods brought into existence represent a mase where, if and when the citizens dare to enter, in search of salvation, are certain to be devoured. The methods and machinery representing a grand pyramid of pyramids need an emergency surgical intervention inorder to save democracy.

Despite the amendments incorporated into the Civil Procedure Code by the Amending Act of 1999, speedy Justice remains as elusive as ever, and increasingly held a captive of an indisciplined judicial system. It has neither an effective supervision, nor an internalised system of self-regulation and discipline.

In sum, the sise of government is growing, distancing itself from the people, the enervation of state leading to a loss of trust among the people. As Dame O' Neil has observed,.delivering the Lord Reith Memorial Lecture, (London 2003); "when trust is lost, we can't even get up in the morning feeling safe".

6.5. Reclaim the Civil Society

Bulwark of democracy

Traditionally, it was believed that the civil society functions as the bulwark of democracy. Intellectuals as the 'conscience-keepers' of the nation had kept up a vigil over the manner and methods of functioning of democracy, and the instrumentalities of state.

Political functionaries were always alert to the public statements emanating from the institutions of the civil society such as the intellectuals, the professional groups and the media for such statements educate the public and shape public opinion. The strength and status of the civil society emanated from the fact that they operated on the basis of well meaning, non-partisan, independent views, a true creative critic, unmindful of the power-wielders of the society. Their views were neither coloured nor motivated by personal gain. Thus the civil society remained and operated as the countervailing force.

While it is an essential requisite for the harmonious functioning of institutions, it is even more important that the gravity of constitutional democracy is held firmly in the polity, the society. This is the vital function of the civil society in a democracy. The institutions of civil society have grown in numbers and range since Independence, and played a commendable role in strengthening participative democracy. The ignited movement for the restoration of democracy led by Lok Nayak J.P, stands out as a stellar example. But the institutions of civil society seem to be losing some of their inherent strengths, leading to a percolation of some weaknesses. As a part of redefining the role of the state, many large Government Organised Non-Governmental Organisations (GONGOs) have sprouted, and many non-governmental initiatives got converted into extended units of the state bureaucracy.

During the post-Independence phase, however, intellectuals in India started putting on 'partisan-caps', on several occasions, becoming in the process, captives of political organisations, enjoying the fruits of '*subserviance*'. There is an urgent and imperative need for reclaiming the civil society inorder to protect, sustain and strengthen constitutional democracy in India. The need for such a reclamation is even greater in the communities engaged in democratisation. Social audit emerges as a powerful tool in the hands of civil society, not to find fault with the institutions of the state, nor to assume the role of a super-cop, but as the best mechanism to (a) prevent abuses of power, (b) provide feedback, and as a built-in Management Information System.

Indian democracy is waiting for its **Tryst with Destiny**. The Constitution represents a high-yielding variety (HYV) of seed; a gift of the freedom-movement. The HYV represents the vision of a developed India, for participative democracy, accelerated development and good governance. The HYV, like any other seed, has the potential to take roots, derive nourishment and deliver the yield. The 'natural' process can be enriched by proper soil, fertiliser, pesticide and water management, and weeding operations. Nature demonstrates that a tiny seed can crack even a black-granite.

Managing the vision of India calls for creative leadership in sustaining, nurturing, harvesting and enriching the Constitution for the progression of Indian society, for generations to come, to pass on the heritage, duly enriched, to the coming generations. The constitution has the potential to convert India from being the numerically largest democracy in to a great democracy.

References

1. Aurobinod Ghosh, Introduction to Bala Gangadhar Tilak : His Writings and Speaches, Ganesh and Co. Madras 19 pxv.
2. Jawaharlal Nehru. Constitution and Constituent Assembly ibid p. 56.
3. S. Radhakrishnan. Constitution and Constituent Assembly ibid p. 61.
4. James Madison. The Federalist Papers No. 10 (1788) Hammondnorth, UK, Penguin 1987.

5. BR Ambedkar Constitution and Constituent Assembly ibid p.
6. Vivekananda, Swamy, The complete works of Swami Vivekananda, RK Misison, Kolkata, Vol. II, 11th Edition 1968.
7. Haq Mahbubul Reflections on Human Development, New Delhi, Oxford University Press 1999, p. 77.
8. Margaret Mead.
9. Minoo Masani, Powers of the President, Freedom Fist, July 1987, p. 53.

Annexure - 1
Directive Principles

In sum they are : (38) promotion of welfare of the people, by securing and protecting as effectively as it may a social order in which justice, social,

economic and political, shall inform all the institutions of the national life; (39) securing, men and women equally, the right to an adequate means of livelihood; distribution of ownership and control of the material resources as best to subserve the common good; economic system not to result in the concentration of wealth and means of production to the common detriment; equal pay for equal work, for both men and women; protection against abuse of health and strength of workers, and the tender age of children; that children are given opportunities and facilities to develop in a healthy manner and in conditions of freedom and dignity, that childhood and youth are protected against exploitation, and against moral and material abandonment; (40) organization of village Panchayats; (41) effective provisions for securing the right to work, to education and to public assistance in cases of unemployment, old age, sickness and disablement; (42) provision for just and humane conditions of work, and for maternity relief; (43) secure a living wage, to all workers agricultural, industrial or otherwise, conditions of work ensuring a decent standard of life and full enjoyment of leisure and social and cultural opportunities; (43 A) secure the participation of workers in the management . . . in industry; (44) secure a uniform civil code throughout the territory of India; (45) free and compulsory education within ten years of all children until 14 years of age; (46) promotion of educational and economic interests of the Scheduled Castes, Schedule Tribes and other weaker sections; (47) raising the level of nutrition, improvement of public health; prohibition of intoxicating drugs; (48) organization of agricultural and animal husbandry on modern and scientific lines and prohibition of cow slaughter; (48 A) protection and improvement of environment and safeguarding of forests and wild life; (49) protection of monuments; (50) separation of judiciary from executive; and, promotion of international peace and security.

Annexure - 2

Fundamental Rights

Vested interests? Equality before law (14); prohibition of discrimination on grounds of religion, race, caste, sex or place of birth (15), equality of opportunity in matters of public employment (16); abolition of untouchability (17); abolition of titles (18); right to freedom of speech and expression, assemble peacefully, form association or unions, and to move freely throughout the territory of India (19); protection in respect of conviction of offences (20); protection of life and personal liberty (21); protection against arrest and detention (22); prohibition of traffic in human beings and forced labour (23); prohibition of employment of children in factories (24); Freedom of conscience and free profession, practice and propagation of religion (25); Freedom to manage religious (27); freedom as to attendance at religious worship in certain educational institutions (28);

protection of interests of minorities (29); and right of minorities to establish and administer educational institutions (30), and, right to constitutional remedies for enforcement of rights conferred by Part III of the Constitution (32), are the Fundamental Rights of Citizens Conferred upon by the Constitution.

Annexure - 3

Fundamental Duties

The 42nd Amendment (1976) was brought about in accordance with the recommendations of the Swaran Singh Committee, bringing our Constitution in line with Art 29(1) of the Universal Declaration of Human Rights, and the Constitutions of Japan, China and USSR.

These duties incorporated in Art 51A are addressed to the citizen, without any sanction for their violation.

These duties encompass (a) to abide by the Constitution and respect its ideal and institutions, the National Flag and the National Anthem; (b) to cherish and follow the noble ideals which inspired our national struggle for freedom; (c) to uphold and protect and sovereignty, unity and integrity of India; (d) to defend the country and render national service when called upon to do so; (e) to promote harmony and the spirit of common brotherhood amongst all the people of India, transcending religious, linguistic and regional or sectional diversities; to renounce practices derogatory to the dignity of women; (f) to value and preserve the rich heritage of our composite culture; (g) to protect and improve the natural environment including forests, lakes, rivers and the wild life, and to have compassion for living creatures; (h) to develop the scientific temper, humanism and the spirit of inquiry and reform; (i) to safeguard public property and to abjure violence; (j) to strive towards excellence in all spheres of individual and collective activity, so that the nation constantly rises to higher levels of endeavour and achievement.

INDEX